D0604650

Donna Kooler's Cross-Stitch Designs

333 Patterns for Ready-to-Stitch Projects

Donna Kooler's Cross-Stitch Designs

333 Patterns for Ready-to-Stitch Projects

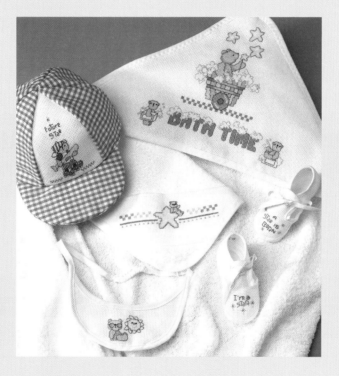

Sterling Publishing Co, Inc., New York
A Sterling/Chapelle Book

Kooler Design Studio

President: *Donna Kooler*
Executive Vice President: *Linda Gillum*
Vice President: *Priscilla Timm*

Editor: *Priscilla Timm*
Contributing Editors: *Deanna Hall West, Arlis Johnson*
Charters: *Deanna Hall West, Lennea LaHammedieu*
Designers: *Linda Gillum, Barbara Baatz, Sandy Orton, Jorja Hernandez, Nancy Rossi, Pam Johnson, Robin Kingsley, Holly DeFount, Donna Yuen*
Design Assistants: *Sara Angle, Anita Forfang, Virginia Hanley-Rivett, Marsha Hinkson, Lori Patton, Char Randolph, Giana Shaw*
Proof Readers: *Arlis Johnson, Anita Forfang*

Photographer: *Dianne Woods, Berkeley, California*
Photo Stylists: *Donna Kooler, Deanna Hall West*
Cross-stitch Program: *Pattern Maker for Cross stitch Hobby Ware, Inc. Indianapolis, IN*

Chapelle Ltd.

Owner: Jo Packham

Editor: Linda Orton

Welcome to Kooler Design Studio's first book of patterns especially designed to be used on premade articles.

These designs were created for when you want the perfect baby gift, a mug for your favorite neighbor, a bookmark for your mother, or a token of friendship for someone special. In this collection you will find the perfect choice which can easily be stitched in a few hours or days and finished without any sewing! Quick and easy–what a boon this is in the fast-paced world where time has become a precious commodity.

With our 333 designs, you can create an endless array of beautiful projects.

Let your imagination run wild and enjoy!

Dedicated to R. Scott Horton for his patience and knowledge.

A special thanks to Adam Original, Charles Craft, Crafter's Pride, Jeanette Crews, MCG Textiles, and Zweigart for their ready-to-stitch products.

Library of Congress Cataloging-in-Publication Data Available

10 9 8 7 6 5 4 3 2 1

A Sterling/Chapelle Book

Published by Sterling Publishing Company, Inc.
387 Park Avenue South, New York, NY 10016
© 2000 by Chapelle Ltd.
Distributed in Canada by Sterling Publishing
% Canadian Manda Group, One Atlantic Avenue, Suite 105
Toronto, Ontario, Canada M6K 3E7
Distributed in Great Britain and Europe by Cassell PLC
Wellington House, 125 Strand, London WC2R 0BB, England
Distributed in Australia by Capricorn Link (Australia) Pty Ltd.
P.O. Box 6651, Baulkham Hills, Business Centre, NSW 2153, Australia
Printed in China
All Rights Reserved

Sterling ISBN 0-8069-3796-3

Every effort has been made to ensure that all of the information in this book is accurate. However, due to differing conditions, tools, and individual skills, the publisher cannot be responsible for any injuries, losses, and/or other damages which may result from the use of the information in this book.

If you have any questions or comments, please contact:

Chapelle Ltd., Inc.
P.O. Box 9252
Ogden, UT 84409

Phone: (801) 621-2777
FAX: (801) 621-2788
e-mail: Chapelle@aol.com

Table of Contents

General Instructions
6–7

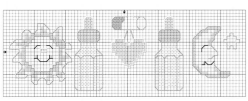

Designs for Baby
8–25

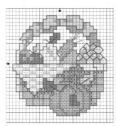

Designs for
Jar Covers
60–73

Designs for Mugs
74–85

Designs for Pillows
26–37

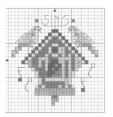

Designs for
Small
Accessories
86–99

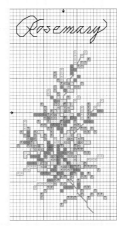

Designs for
Bookmarks
100–113

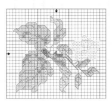

Designs for
Table Linens
38–49

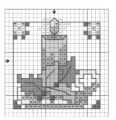

Designs for
Christmas
114–125

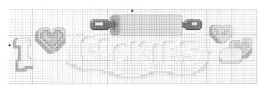

Designs for Towels
50–59

Alphabets
126

Metric Equivalency Chart
127

Index
128

General Instructions

Introduction
333 patterns for ready-to-stitch projects have been included in *Donna Kooler's Cross-Stitch Designs* and in most cases require very minimal or no construction.

Fabric for Cross-stitch
Counted cross-stitch is worked on even-weave fabrics, such as Aida. These fabrics are manufactured primarily for counted-thread embroidery, and are woven with the same number of vertical as horizontal threads per inch.

Because the number of threads in the fabric is equal in each direction, each stitch will be the same size. The number of threads per inch in even-weave fabrics determines the size of a finished design.

Number of Floss Strands
The number of strands used per stitch varies, depending on the fabric used. Generally, the rule to follow for cross-stitching is three strands of floss on Aida 11, two strands on Aida 14, one or two strands on Aida 18 (depending on desired thickness of stitches), and one strand on Hardanger 22.

For backstitching, use one strand on all fabrics. When completing a french knot, use two strands and one wrap on all fabrics, unless otherwise directed.

Finished Design Size
To determine the size of the finished design, divide the stitch count by the number of threads per inch of fabric. When the design is stitched over two threads, divide stitch count by half the threads per inch. For example, if a design with a stitch count

of 120 width and 250 length were stitched on a 28-count linen over two threads, use the following formula: 120 (stitch width) divided by 14 (stitches per inch) = 8⅝" and 250 divided by 14 = 17⅞", to determine the finished design size of 8⅝" x 17⅞".

Preparing Fabric
Cut fabric at least 3" larger on all sides than the finished design size to ensure enough space for desired assembly. To prevent fraying, whipstitch or machine-zigzag along the raw edges or apply liquid fray preventive.

Needles for Cross-stitch
Blunt needles should slip easily through the fabric holes without piercing fabric threads. For fabric with 11 or fewer threads per inch, use a tapestry needle size 24; for 14 threads per inch, use a tapestry needle size 24 or 26; for 18 or more threads per inch, use a tapestry needle size 26. Never leave the needle in the design area of the fabric. It may leave rust or a permanent impression on the fabric.

Floss
All numbers and color names on the codes represent the DMC brand of floss. Use 18" lengths of floss. For best coverage, separate the strands and dampen with a wet sponge. Then put together the number of strands required for the fabric used.

Centering Design
Fold the fabric in half horizontally, then vertically. Place a pin in the fold point to mark the center. Locate the center of the design on the graph. To help in centering the designs, arrows are provided at left-center and top-center. Begin stitching all designs at the center point of the graph and fabric.

Securing Floss

Insert needle up from the underside of the fabric at starting point. Hold 1" of thread behind the fabric and stitch over it, securing with the first few stitches. To finish thread, run under four or more stitches on the back of the design. Never knot floss, unless working on clothing.

Another method of securing floss is the waste knot. Knot floss and insert needle down from the right top side of the fabric about 1" from design area. Work several stitches over the thread to secure. Cut off the knot later.

Carrying Floss

To carry floss, weave floss under the previously worked stitches on the back. Do not carry thread across any fabric that is not or will not be stitched. Loose threads, especially dark ones, will show through the fabric.

Cleaning Finished Design

When stitching is finished, soak the fabric in cold water with a mild soap for five to ten minutes. Rinse well and roll in a towel to remove excess water. Do not wring. Place the piece face down on a dry towel and iron on a warm setting until the fabric is dry.

Cross-stitch (XS)

Stitches are done in a row or, if necessary, one at a time in an area.

1. Insert needle up between woven threads at A.

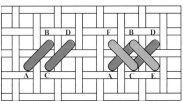

2. Go down at B, the opening diagonally across from A.

3. Come up at C and go down at D, etc.

4. To complete the top stitches creating an "X", come up at E and go down at B, come up at C and go down at F, etc. All top stitches should lie in the same direction.

Backstitch (BS)

1. Insert needle up between woven threads at A.

2. Go down at B, one opening to the right.

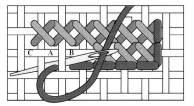

3. Come up at C.

4. Go down at A, one opening to the right.

French Knot (FK)

1. Insert needle up between woven threads at A, using one strand of embroidery floss.

2. Loosely wrap floss once around needle.

3. Go down at B, the opening across from A. Pull floss taut as needle is pushed down through fabric.

4. Carry floss across back of work between knots.

Designs for Baby

Pink Gingham hooded bath towel (as shown on page 9)
Stitch Count: 116 width x 78 length
left

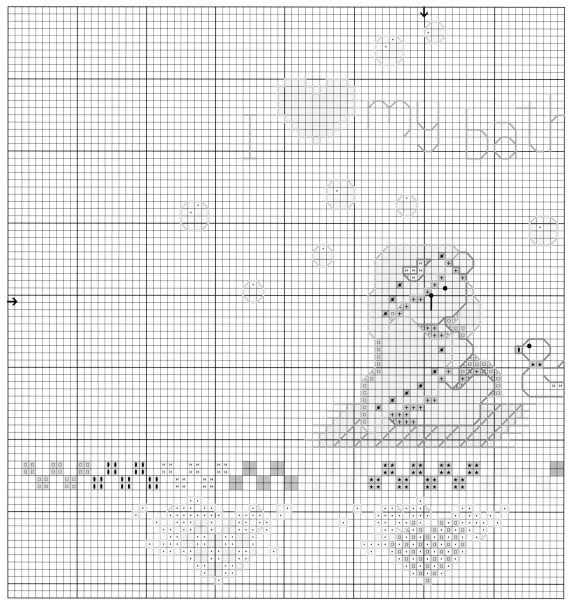

Flower mitten
(as shown on page 9)
Stitch Count: 13 width x 19 length

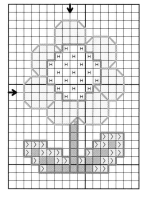

DMC Floss				
X st	X st	BS	BS	FK
· White	818	⌐ 309	⌐ 798	● 310
★ 210	913	⌐ 310	⌐ 799	
309	945	⌐ 335	⌐ 910	
335	› 955	⌐ 400	⌐ 958	
+ 402	* 958	⌐ 414	⌐ 3826	
H 745	964			
746	□ 3326			
800	3824			
809				

10

right

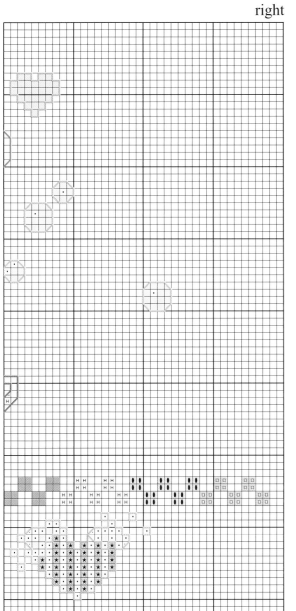

Vine Flower bonnet (right side)
(as shown on page 9)
Stitch Count: 21 width x 32 length

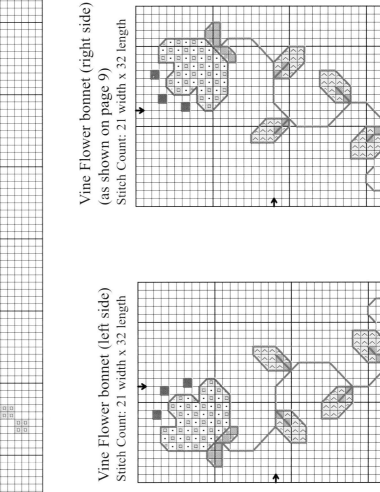

Vine Flower bonnet (left side)
Stitch Count: 21 width x 32 length

Bear mitten
(as shown on page 9)
Stitch Count: 13 width x 15 length

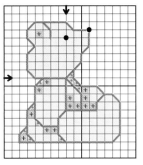

Heart bootie
(as shown on page 8)
Stitch Count: 11 width x 13 length

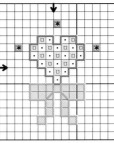

Bear bootie
(as shown on page 8)
Stitch Count: 13 width x 13 length

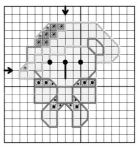

11

pocket bib
Stitch Count: 41 width x 45 length

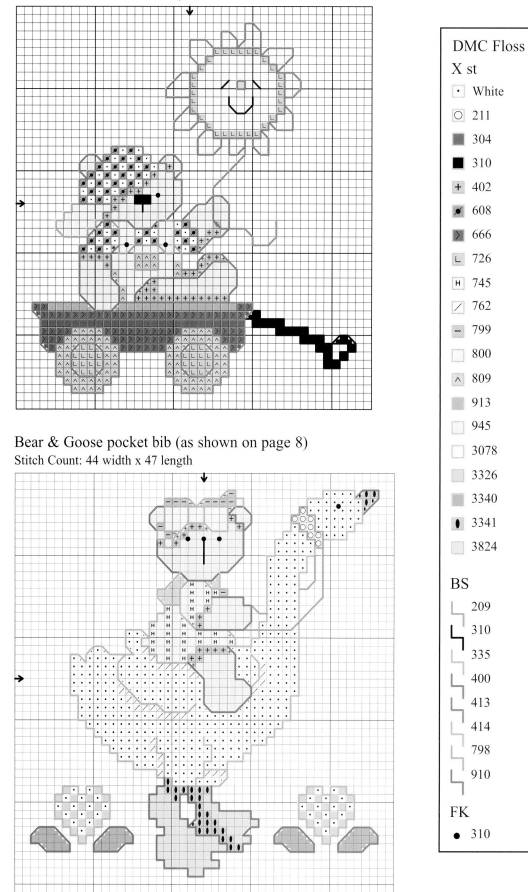

Bear & Goose pocket bib (as shown on page 8)
Stitch Count: 44 width x 47 length

DMC Floss	
X st	
·	White
○	211
■	304
■	310
+	402
	608
▷	666
L	726
H	745
/	762
−	799
	800
^	809
	913
	945
	3078
	3326
	3340
●	3341
	3824

BS	
	209
	310
	335
	400
	413
	414
	798
	910

FK	
●	310

Bear cup (as shown on page 8)
Stitch Count: 78 width x 26 length

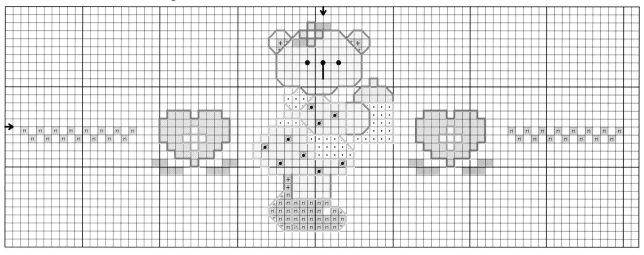

I'm a Star bootie (as shown on page 17)
Stitch Count: 18 width x 13 length

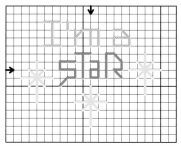

Bear & Flower round bib (as shown on page 9)
Stitch Count: 35 width x 40 length

A Star is Born bootie (as shown on page 17)
Stitch Count: 22 width x 17 length

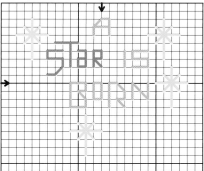

DMC Floss

X st		X st		BS		BS		FK	
·	White		913	⌐	209	⌐	350	●	310
	211		945	⌐	309	⌐	798		
✎	335	>	955	⌐	310		5282		
+	402	n	959	⌐	335				
⏊	743		964	⌐	400				
	745		3326	⌐	414				
○	746		3824	⌐	910				

bootie
Stitch Count: 7 width x 9 length

White hooded bath towel (as shown on page 17)
Stitch Count: 110 width x 93 length
left

right

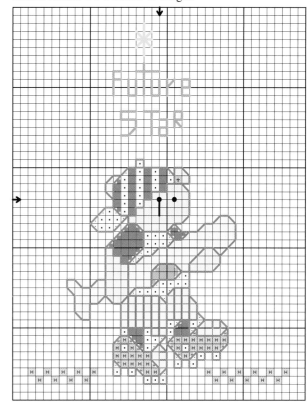

Blue Gingham ball cap (as shown on page 17)
Stitch Count: 34 width x 45 length

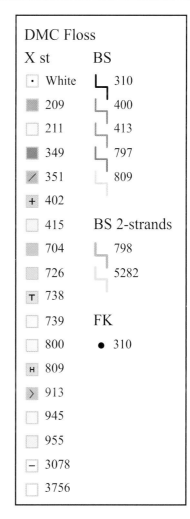

DMC Floss		
X st	**BS**	
· White	⌐	310
209		400
211		413
349		797
╱ 351		809
+ 402		
415	**BS 2-strands**	
704		798
726		5282
T 738		
739	**FK**	
800	●	310
H 809		
❯ 913		
945		
955		
− 3078		
3756		

cup
Stitch Count: 74 width x 23 length

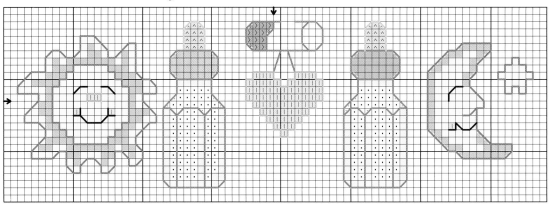

Star & Bear burp towel (as shown on page 17)
Stitch Count: 69 width x 19 length

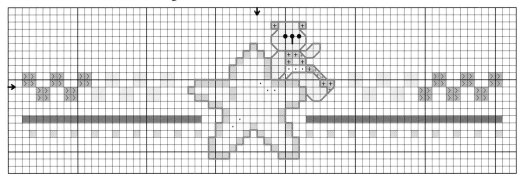

Sun & Bear visor (as shown on page 17)
Stitch Count: 24 width x 18 length

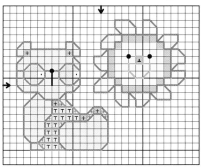

ball cap
Stitch Count: 24 width x 41 length

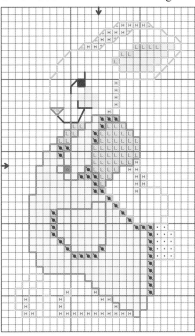

DMC Floss				
X st	X st	X st	BS	BS
· White	726	o 958	309	3341
210	746	959	310	
■ 310	799	T 964	400	FK
350	800	3078	413	• 310
+ 402	> 913	3708	435	
415	945	3713	602	
I 605	955	^ 3824	797	
H 677	L 957		958	

Hearts & Flowers hooded towel (as shown on page 19)
Stitch Count: 175 width x 20 length

left

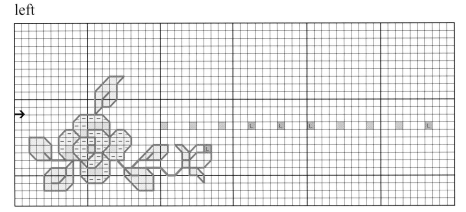

center

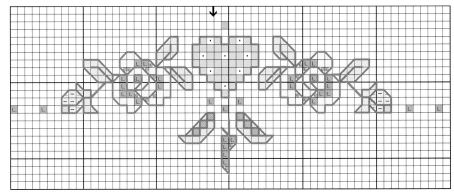

right

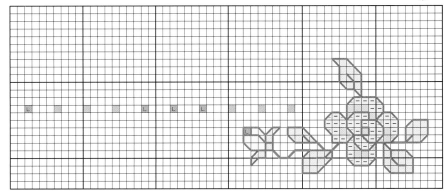

Hearts & Flowers bath mitt (as shown on page 19)
Stitch Count: 71 width x 17 length

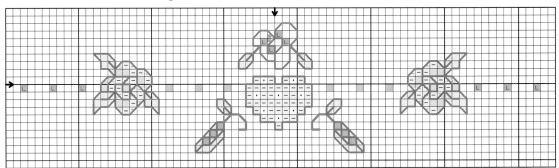

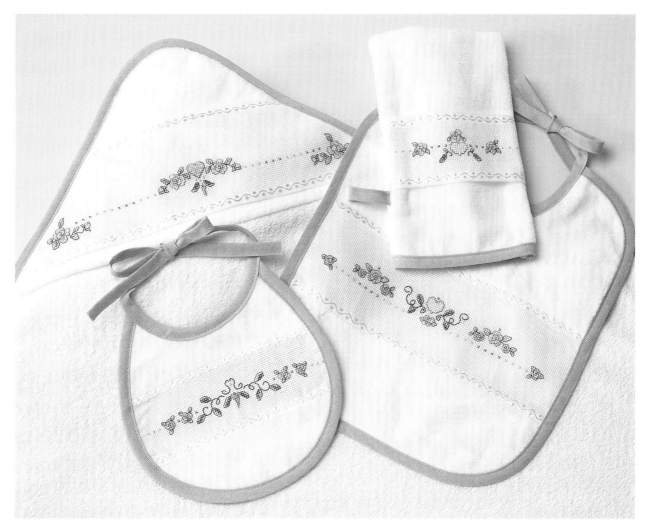

DMC Floss	
X st	
·	White
☐	745
▨	799
−	818
▨	913
☐	955
▨	3326
L	3825
BS	
└	309
└	910
└	3826
BS 2-strands	
└	911

Hearts & Flowers round bib (as shown above)
Stitch Count: 99 width x 15 length
left

right

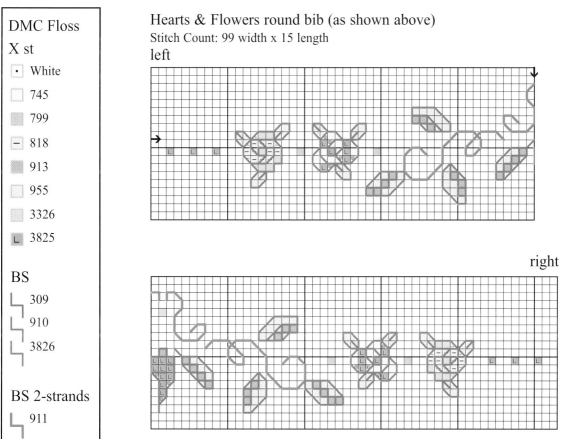

19

Hearts & Flowers square bib (as shown on page 19)
Stitch Count: 136 width x 16 length

left

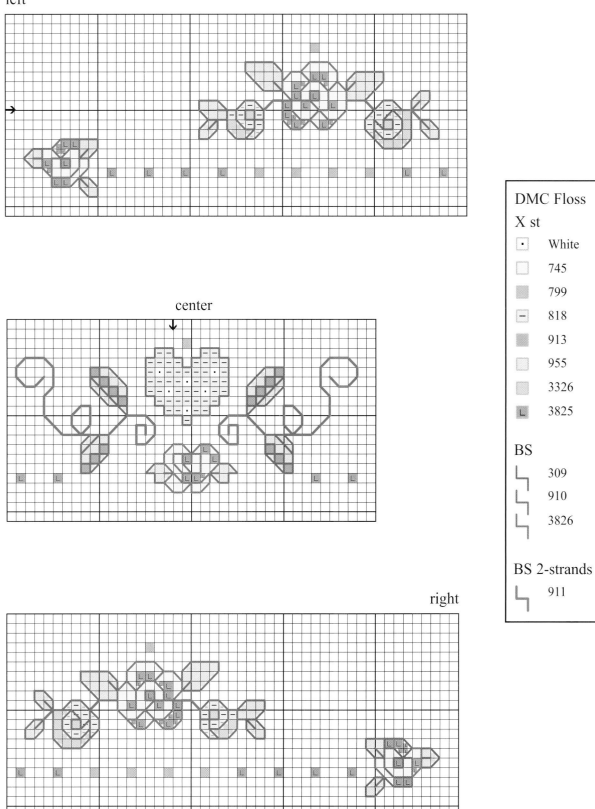

center

right

DMC Floss

X st

·	White
☐	745
▦	799
–	818
▨	913
☐	955
▨	3326
L	3825

BS

⌐	309
⌐	910
⌐	3826

BS 2-strands

⌐	911

bath towel
Stitch Count: 76 width x 64 length

bootie
Stitch Count: 11 width x 17 length

mitten
Stitch Count: 21 width x 15 length

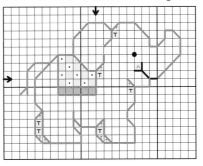

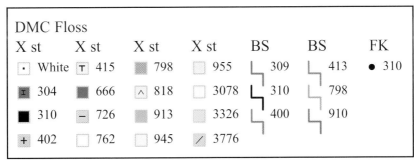

DMC Floss						
X st	X st	X st	X st	BS	BS	FK
· White	T 415	▓ 798	░ 955	└ 309	└ 413	● 310
I 304	▓ 666	∧ 818	□ 3078	└ 310	└ 798	
■ 310	– 726	▓ 913	░ 3326	└ 400	└ 910	
+ 402	□ 762	░ 945	/ 3776			

21

numbers

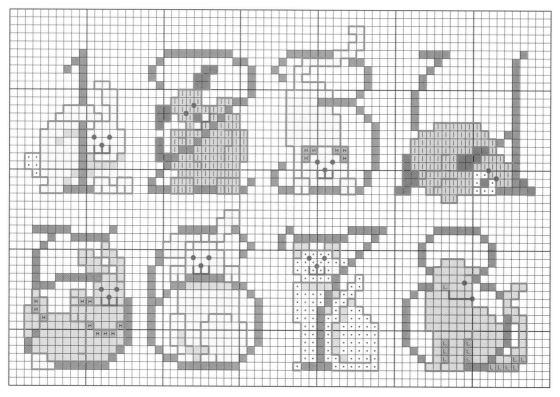

bib
Stitch Count: 34 width x 35 length

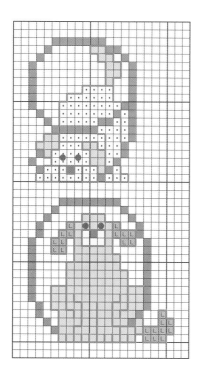

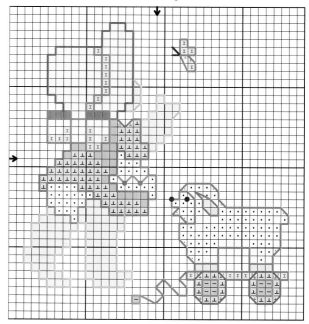

22

Stitch Count: 64 width x 60 length

Stitch Count: 39 width x 36 length

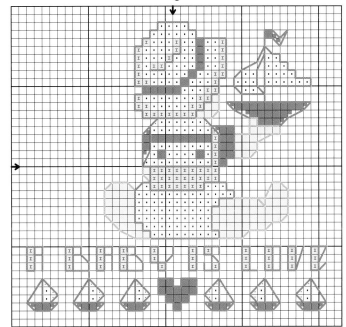

DMC Floss

X st		X st		BS		FK	
·	White		745	⌐	300	●	309
■	300	⊥	776	⌐	309	●	3371
L	301		819	⌐	322		
■	322		899	⌐	349		
■	349	■	912	⌐	413		
I	402		948	⌐	912		
	415	–	954	⌐	3371		
H	435	I	3325	⌐	3778		
	437	■	3371				
	739		3756				
	742						

Stitch Count: 47 width x 46 length

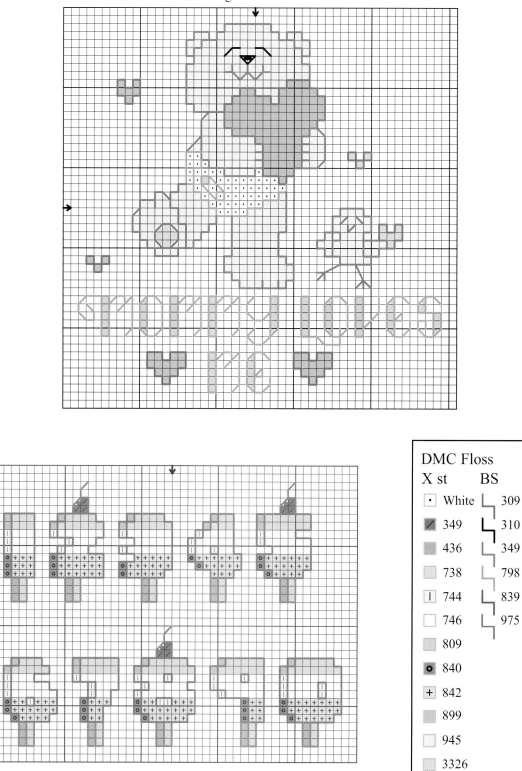

DMC Floss

X st		BS	
·	White	L	309
◢	349	L	310
	436	L	349
	738	L	798
I	744	L	839
	746	L	975
	809		
◉	840		
+	842		
	899		
	945		
	3326		

24

Stitch Count: 70 width x 49 length

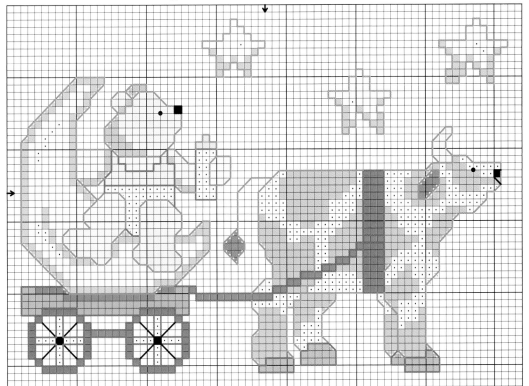

Stitch Count: 48 width x 57 length

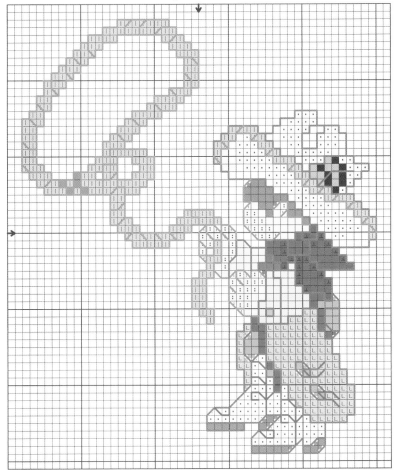

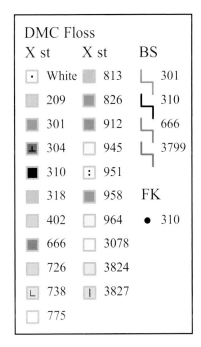

DMC Floss		
X st	X st	BS
· White	▨ 813	└ 301
▨ 209	▨ 826	⌐ 310
▨ 301	▨ 912	⌐ 666
⊥ 304	☐ 945	⌐ 3799
■ 310	: 951	
▨ 318	▨ 958	FK
▨ 402	☐ 964	● 310
▨ 666	☐ 3078	
▨ 726	☐ 3824	
L 738	I 3827	
☐ 775		

25

Designs for Pillows

To the Beach pillow (as shown on page 27)
Stitch Count: 81 width x 71 length

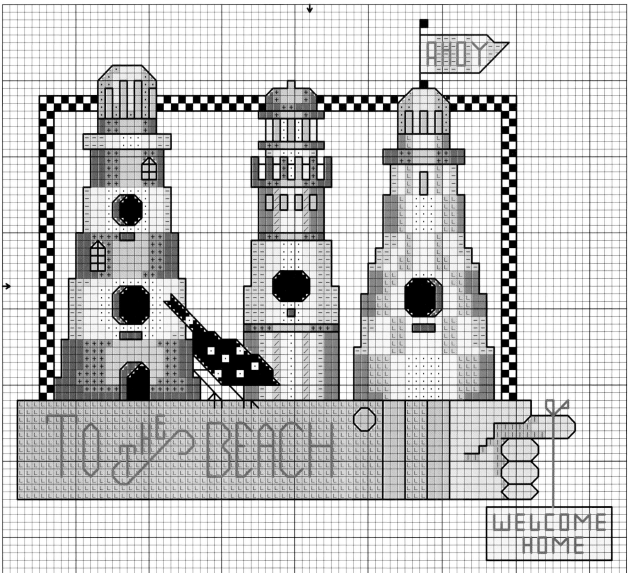

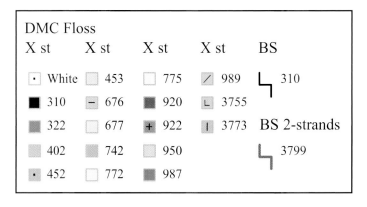

DMC Floss				
X st	X st	X st	X st	BS
· White	453	775	/ 989	310
310	— 676	920	L 3755	
322	677	+ 922	I 3773	BS 2-strands
402	742	950		3799
· 452	772	987		

Sunflower pillow (as shown on page 26)
Stitch Count: 51 width x 73 length

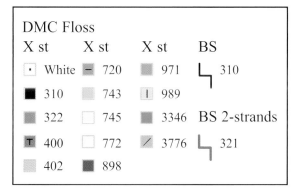

DMC Floss			
X st	X st	X st	BS
· White	– 720	971	⌐ 310
■ 310	743	I 989	
322	745	3346	BS 2-strands
T 400	□ 745	╱ 3776	⌐ 321
402	□ 772		
	■ 898		

Stitch Count: 38 width x 48 length

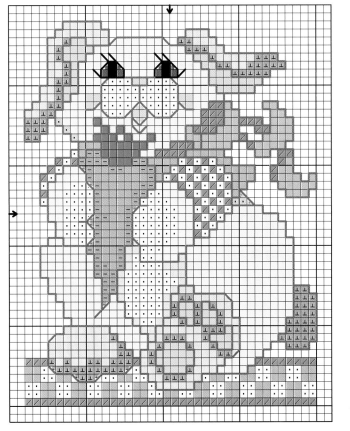

Stitch Count: 36 width x 46 length

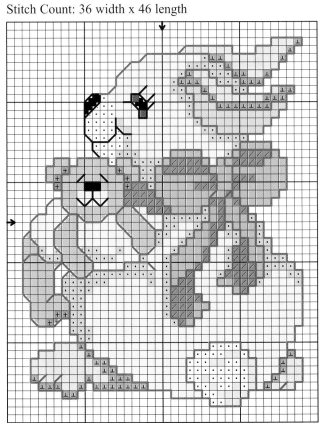

Stitch Count: 41 width x 52 length

DMC Floss		
X st	X st	BS
· White	· 738	⌐ 310
+ 301	739	⌐ 3799
■ 310	− 740	
321	741	
402	743	
⊥ 414	776	
415	826	
433	╱ 958	
700	959	
718		

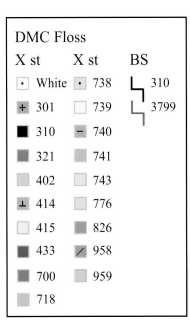

Stitch Count: 69 width x 85 length

DMC Floss			
X st	X st	X st	BS
· White	☐ 744	▨ 3325	⌐ 301
▨ 209	╱ 762	+ 3733	⌐ 310
▨ 301	☐ 772	− 3755	⌐ 825
■ 310	☐ 776		⌐ 3799
▨ 563	L 977		

Stitch Count: 52 width x 45 length

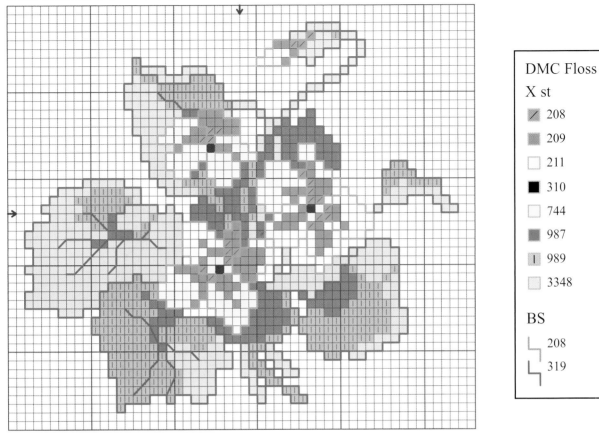

DMC Floss
X st

/	208
	209
	211
■	310
	744
	987
I	989
	3348

BS

| └ | 208 |
| └ | 319 |

Victorian pillow (as shown on page 32)
Stitch Count: 60 width x 83 length

DMC Floss							
X st	X st	X st	X st	X st	X st	BS	BS
· White	■ 319	▮ 603	⁄ 772	– 971	+ 3755	⌐ 208	⌐ 825
■ 208	■ 321	▮ 604	□ 775	▮ 977	■ 3812	⌐ 310	⌐ 900
> 209	■ 322	⁄ 606	▮ 900	⌐ 987	· 3817	⌐ 600	⌐ 986
□ 211	⊥ 502	▮ 742	⊥ 958	▮ 989	■ 3826	⌐ 742	
■ 310	▮ 600	□ 744	▮ 959	· 3689			

Birdhouse pillow (as shown on page 35)
Stitch Count: 58 width x 84 length

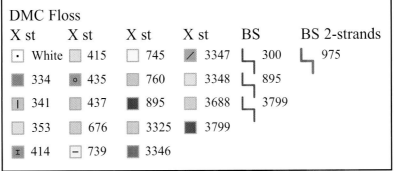

DMC Floss					
X st	X st	X st	X st	BS	BS 2-strands
· White	415	745	/ 3347	└ 300	└ 975
334	o 435	760	3348	└ 895	
I 341	437	895	3688	└ 3799	
353	676	3325	3799		
I 414	− 739	3346			

Stitch Count: 50 width x 45 length

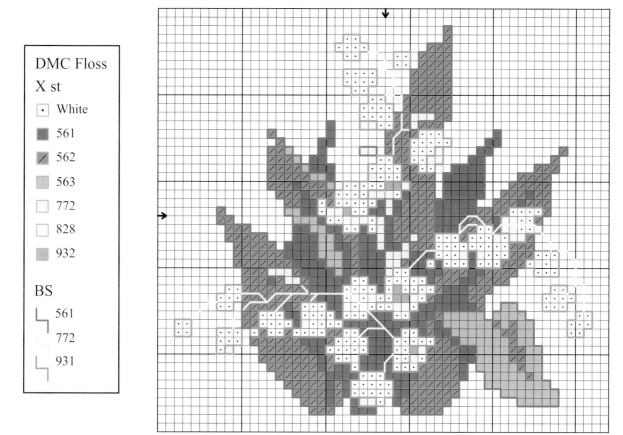

DMC Floss
X st

· White
561
562
563
772
828
932

BS
561
772
931

35

Frog pillow (as shown on page 35)
Stitch Count: 52 width x 76 length

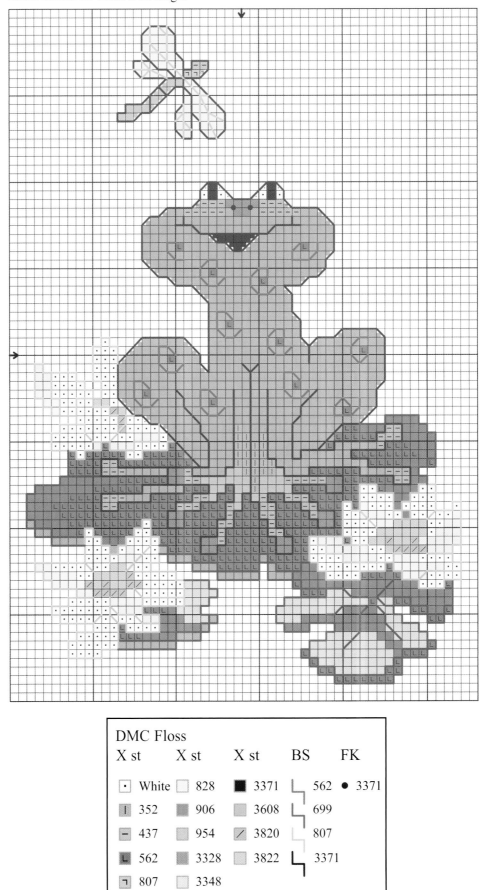

DMC Floss

X st		X st		X st		BS		FK	
·	White		828	■	3371	L	562	●	3371
I	352		906		3608	L	699		
-	437		954	/	3820	L	807		
L	562		3328		3822	L	3371		
¬	807		3348						

Stitch Count: 57 width x 72 length

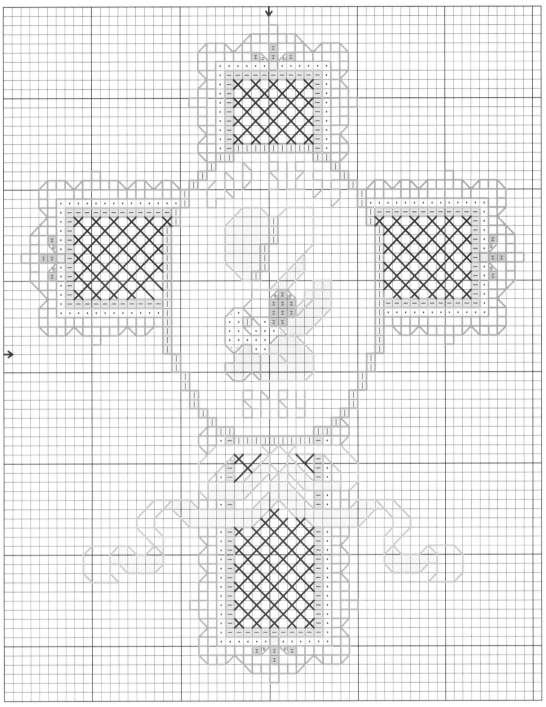

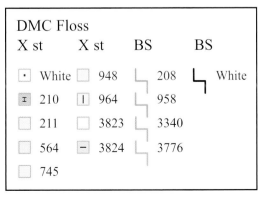

DMC Floss			
X st	X st	BS	BS
· White	948	∟ 208	⌐ White
ェ 210	Ι 964	∟ 958	
211	3823	∟ 3340	
564	− 3824	∟ 3776	
745			

Designs for

Table Linens

Feather place mat (as shown on page 39)
Stitch Count: 64 width x 68 length

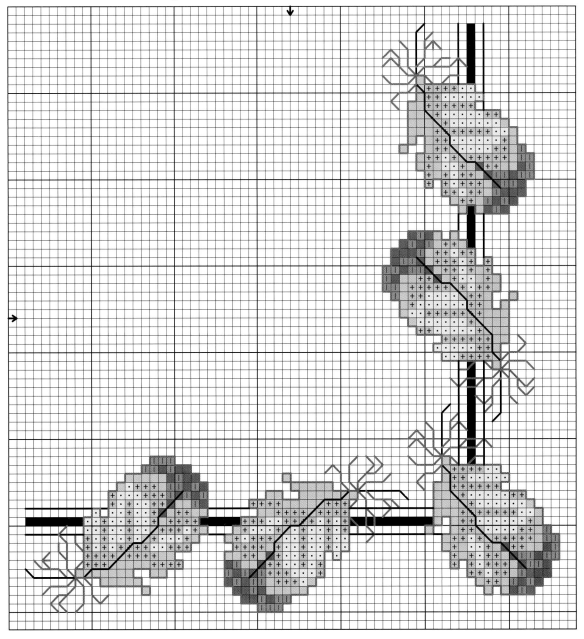

Feather napkin (as shown on page 39)
Stitch Count: 18 width x 22 length

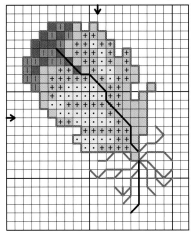

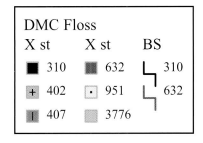

DMC Floss

X st		X st		BS	
■	310	▨	632	⌐	310
+	402	·	951	⌐	632
‖	407	▨	3776		

Stitch Count: 69 width x 69 length

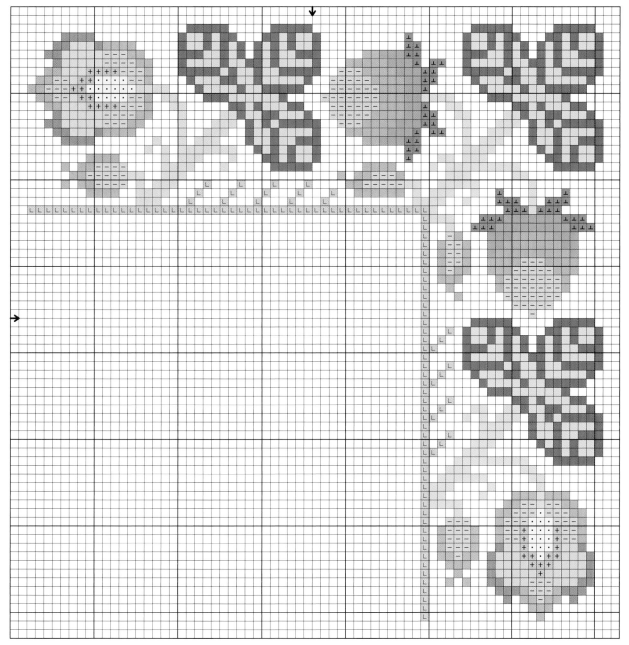

Stitch Count: 34 width x 21 length

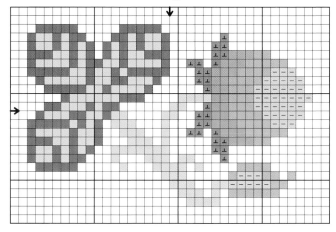

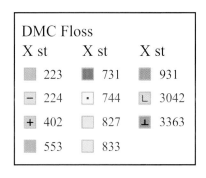

DMC Floss		
X st	X st	X st
223	731	931
224	744	3042
402	827	3363
553	833	

41

Stitch Count: 42 width x 60 length

DMC Floss

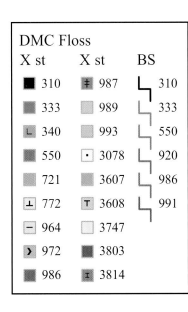

X st		X st		BS	
■	310	‡	987	⌐	310
■	333		989	⌐	333
∟	340		993	⌐	550
■	550	·	3078	⌐	920
	721		3607	⌐	986
⊥	772	T	3608	⌐	991
–	964		3747		
›	972	■	3803		
■	986	⌶	3814		

Pansy place mat (as shown on page 39)
Stitch Count: 39 width x 33 length

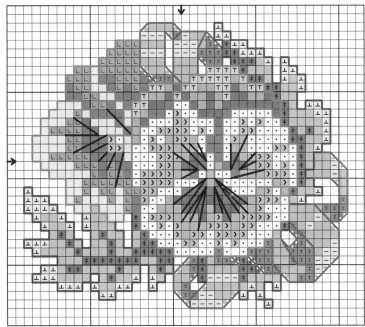

Pansy napkin (as shown on page 39)
Stitch Count: 22 width x 24 length

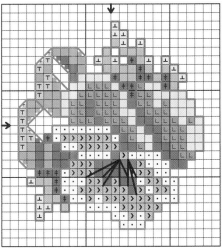

Stitch Count: 16 width x 34 length

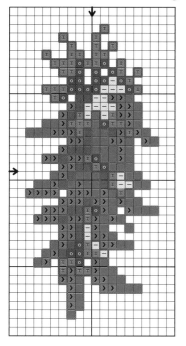

Stitch Count: 37 width x 71 length

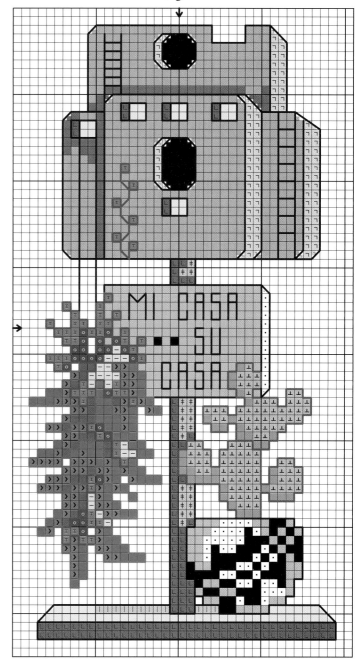

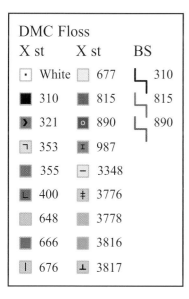

DMC Floss		
X st	X st	BS
· White	677	310
■ 310	815	815
❯ 321	⊙ 890	890
⌐ 353	I 987	
355	− 3348	
╚ 400	‡ 3776	
648	3778	
666	3816	
I 676	⊥ 3817	

Stitch Count: 70 width x 69 length

Stitch Count: 28 width x 24 length

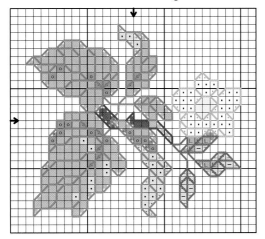

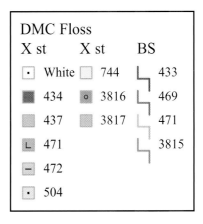

DMC Floss		
X st	X st	BS
· White	☐ 744	⌐ 433
■ 434	⊙ 3816	⌐ 469
▨ 437	▨ 3817	⌐ 471
L 471		⌐ 3815
– 472		
· 504		

44

Butterfly place mat (as shown on page 39)
Stitch Count: 39 width x 51 length

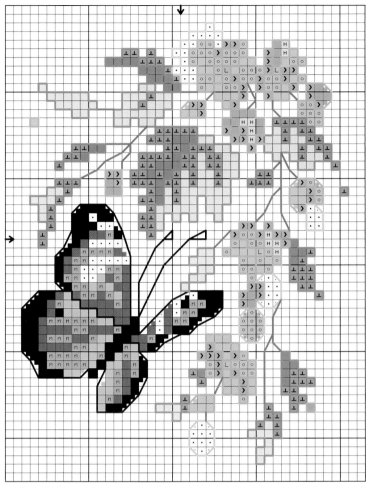

Butterfly napkin
(as shown on page 39)
Stitch Count: 17 width x 19 length

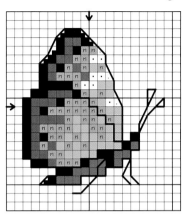

Stitch Count: 28 width x 67 length

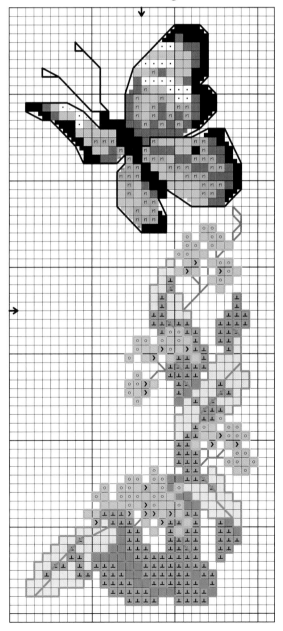

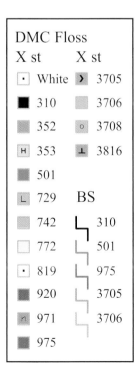

DMC Floss			
X st		X st	
·	White	❭	3705
■	310		3706
	352	o	3708
H	353	⊥	3816
	501		
L	729	**BS**	
	742	⌐	310
	772	⌐	501
·	819	⌐	975
	920	⌐	3705
n	971	⌐	3706
	975		

Stitch Count: 61 width x 62 length

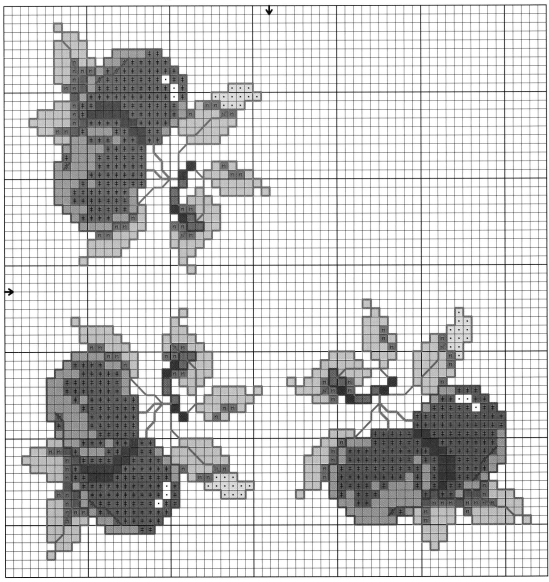

Stitch Count: 16 width x 14 length

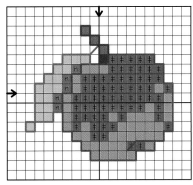

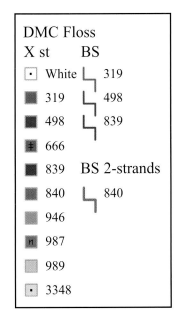

DMC Floss

X st	BS
⊡ White	319
■ 319	498
■ 498	839
‡ 666	
■ 839	BS 2-strands
■ 840	840
■ 946	
n 987	
■ 989	
⊡ 3348	

46

Stitch Count: 30 width x 30 length

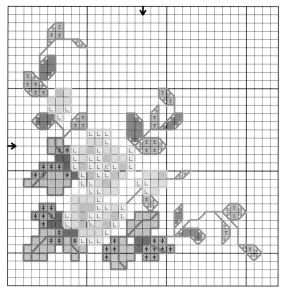

Eat Dessert First place mat (as shown on page 38)
Stitch Count: 38 width x 50 length

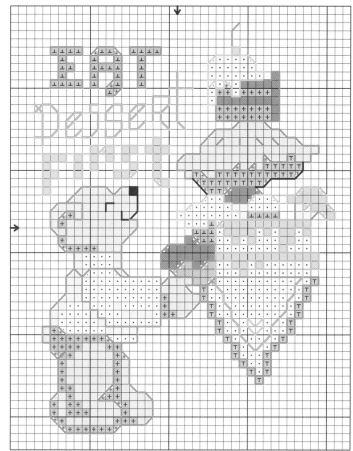

DMC Floss

X st		X st		BS	
·	White		800	⌐	310
	210	T	809		335
■	310	L	818		400
	335	■	905		437
+	402		945		561
	434	⊥	959		905
I	471		3817		3810
‡	502	·	3823		
	561				BS 2-strands
	745			⌐	597
	776				

Stitch Count: 44 width x 29 length

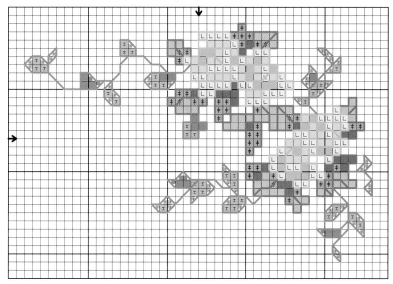

Eat Dessert First napkin
(as shown on page 38)
Stitch Count: 20 width x 18 length

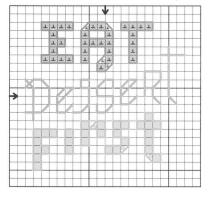

Red Berries place mat (as shown on page 38)
Stitch Count: 65 width x 59 length

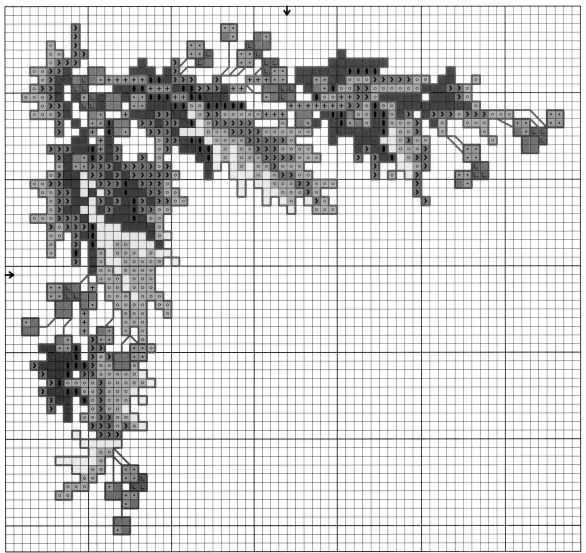

Red Berries napkin
(as shown on page 38)
Stitch Count: 18 width x 17 length

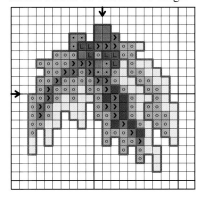

Stitch Count: 42 width x 68 length

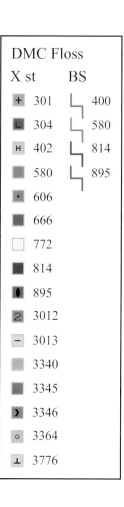

DMC Floss

X st		BS	
+	301	⌐	400
L	304	⌐	580
H	402	⌐	814
	580	⌐	895
•	606		
	666		
	772		
	814		
●	895		
2	3012		
-	3013		
	3340		
	3345		
❯	3346		
o	3364		
⊥	3776		

Designs

for Towels

Violin towel (as shown on page 51)
Stitch Count: 54 width x 30 length

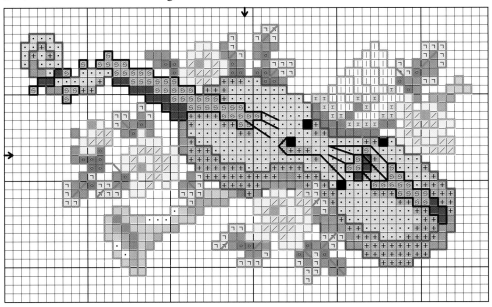

Stitch Count: 71 width x 25 length

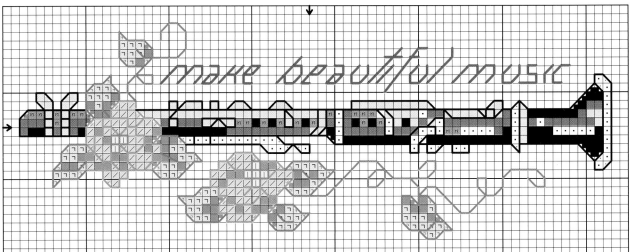

Stitch Count: 75 width x 21 length

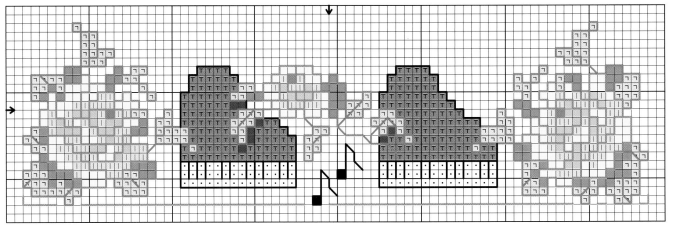

Welcome fingertip towel (as shown on page 51)
Stitch Count: 54 width x 25 length

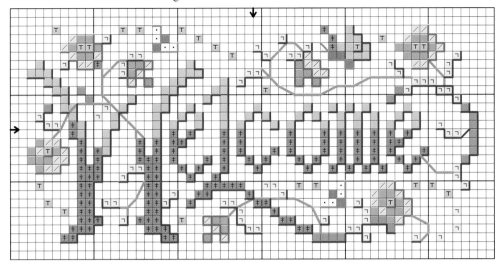

Hibiscus fingertip towel (as shown on page 51)
Stitch Count: 56 width x 28 length

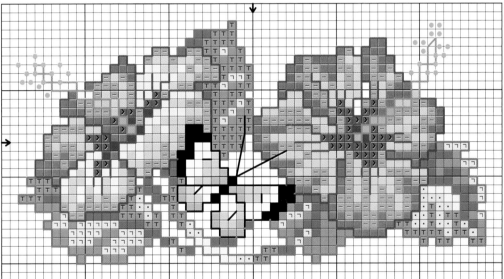

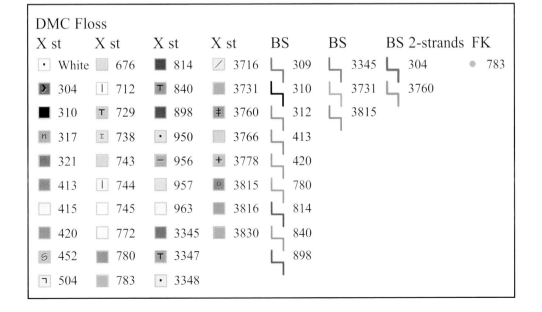

DMC Floss

X st	X st	X st	X st	BS	BS	BS 2-strands	FK
· White	676	■ 814	╱ 3716	└ 309	└ 3345	└ 304	• 783
❯ 304	Ⅰ 712	T 840	3731	└ 310	└ 3731	└ 3760	
■ 310	T 729	898	‡ 3760	312	└ 3815		
n 317	ⅈ 738	· 950	3766	└ 413			
■ 321	743	— 956	+ 3778	└ 420			
413	Ⅰ 744	957	o 3815	└ 780			
415	745	963	3816	└ 814			
420	772	■ 3345	3830	└ 840			
s 452	780	T 3347		└ 898			
ꓘ 504	783	· 3348					

Stitch Count: 51 width x 21 length

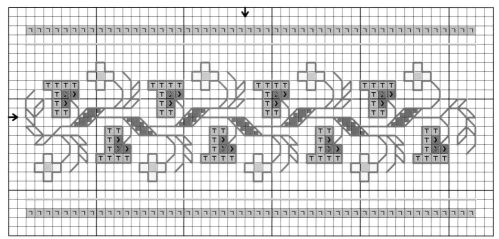

Grapes fingertip towel (as shown on page 51)
Stitch Count: 56 width x 31 length

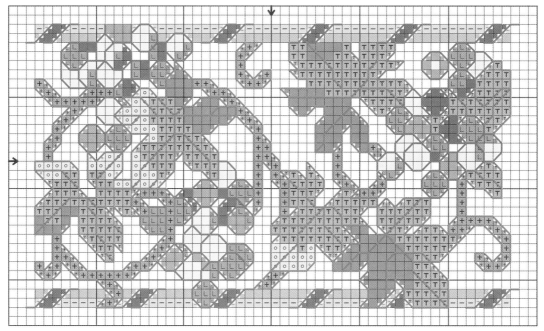

Stitch Count: 58 width x 23 length

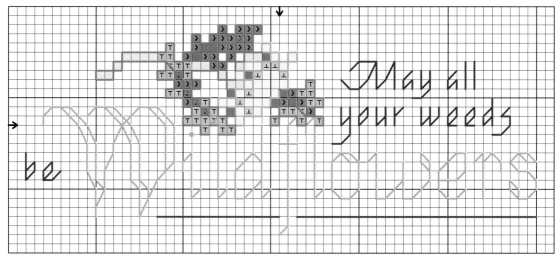

Stitch Count: 80 width x 28 length

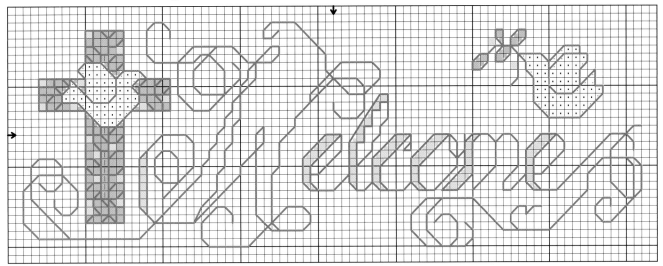

Daisy fingertip towel (as shown on page 51)
Stitch Count: 77 width x 30 length

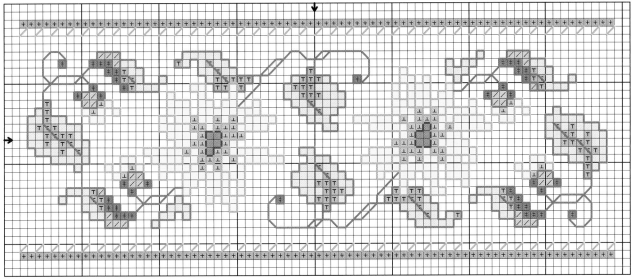

DMC Floss					
X st	X st	X st	X st	BS	FK
· White	⊥ 742	‡ 3012	⌐ 3778	└ 301	● 301
+ 301	744	/ 3013	− 3822	└ 309	
320	797	3326		└ 797	
⌐ 340	800	3345		└ 3345	
➤ 469	○ 834	3348		└ 3371	
553	966	T 3364		└ 3781	
729	∣ 977	3772			

55

Stitch Count: 114 width x 29 length
left

right

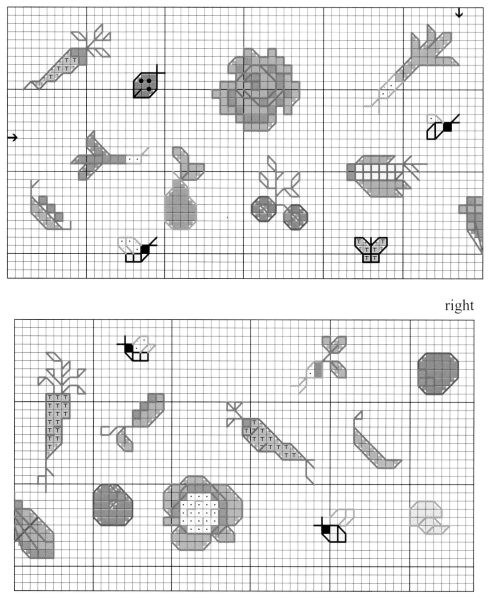

Stitch Count: 62 width x 24 length

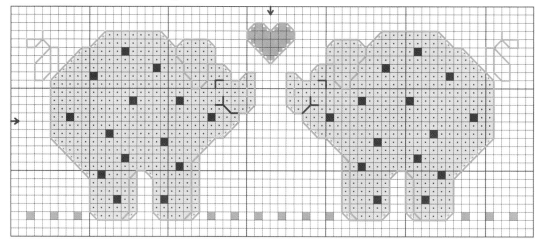

Seasons Greetings fingertip towel (as shown on page 51)
Stitch Count: 72 width x 30 length

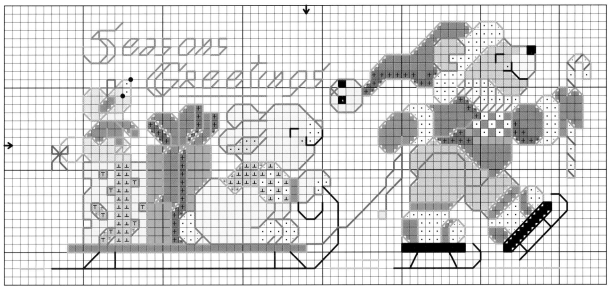

Stitch Count: 64 width x 31 length

DMC Floss						
X st	X st	X st	X st	BS	BS	FK
· White	T 722	966	· 3716	310	961	• 310
■ 310	739	988	3799	317	986	
317	744	− 993	3827	400	996	
+ 321	754	996		700	3799	
400	I 809	3325		809		
553	912	n 3326		816		
606	o 943	| 3341		943		
644	961	⊥ 3608				

Cookies potholder (as shown on page 50)
Stitch Count: 43 width x 41 length

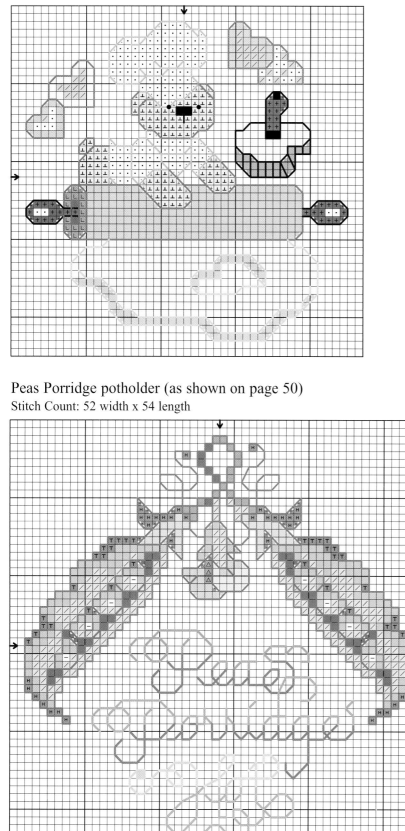

Peas Porridge potholder (as shown on page 50)
Stitch Count: 52 width x 54 length

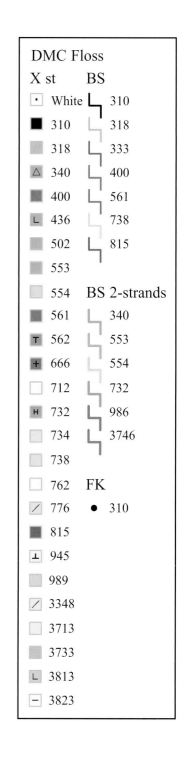

DMC Floss	
X st	**BS**
· White	⌐ 310
■ 310	⌐ 318
318	⌐ 333
△ 340	⌐ 400
400	⌐ 561
L 436	⌐ 738
502	⌐ 815
553	
554	**BS 2-strands**
561	⌐ 340
T 562	⌐ 553
+ 666	⌐ 554
712	⌐ 732
H 732	⌐ 986
734	⌐ 3746
738	
762	**FK**
⁄ 776	● 310
815	
⊥ 945	
989	
⁄ 3348	
3713	
3733	
L 3813	
− 3823	

Cookies kitchen towel (as shown on page 50)
Stitch Count: 96 width x 25 length

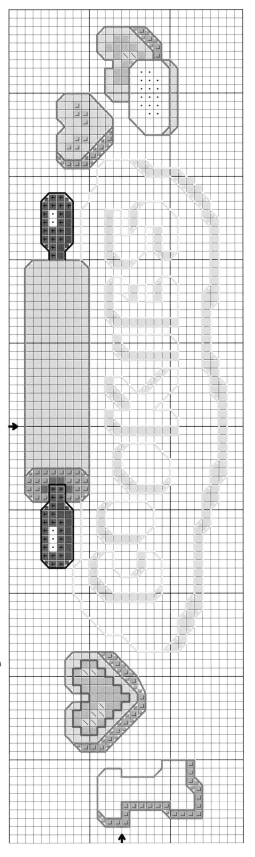

Peas Please kitchen towel (as shown on page 50)
Stitch Count: 83 width x 39 length

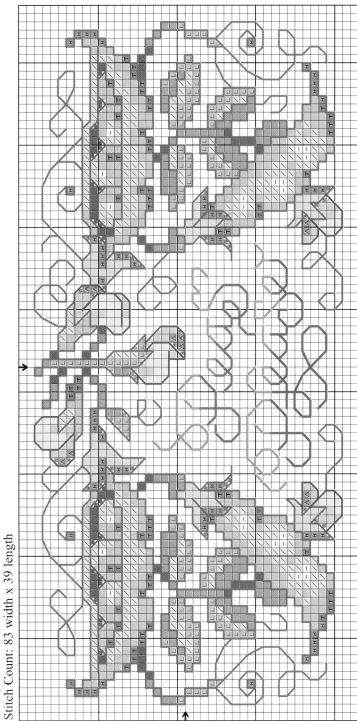

Designs for Jar Covers and Coasters

Apple coaster (as shown on page 61)
Stitch Count: 27 width x 29 length

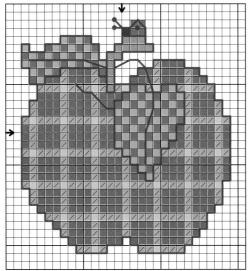

Cherries coaster (as shown on page 61)
Stitch Count: 30 width x 28 length

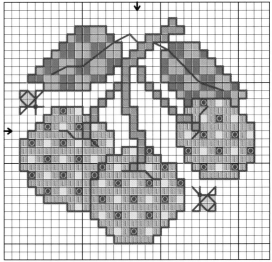

Watermelon jar cover (as shown on page 60)
Stitch Count: 25 width x 28 length

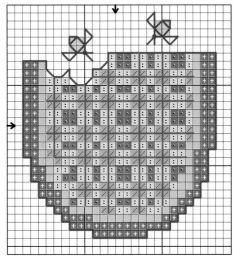

Pear coaster (as shown on page 60)
Stitch Count: 26 width x 27 length

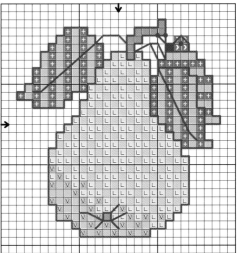

Pumpkin jar cover (as shown on page 61)
Stitch Count: 29 width x 29 length

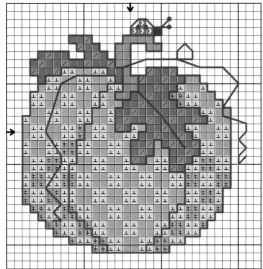

Carrots jar cover (as shown on page 61)
Stitch Count: 25 width x 29 length

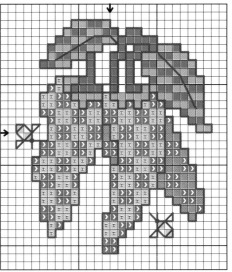

DMC Floss

X st		X st		X st	
·	White	·	746		989
	301	−	760	H	3326
⊙	304		817	V	3340
	309		818		3341
·	349		824	I	3706
/	351		826	⊥	3825
:	353		827		
	552		899	**BS**	
I	602		905	└	304
	604	/	906	└	938
❭	666		907		
‡	720	○	911	**FK**	
	721		938	●	938
	743	·	954		
L	744	➕	987		

Heart jar cover (as shown on page 61)
Stitch Count: 28 width x 28 length

Strawberry jar cover (as shown on page 67)
Stitch Count: 24 width x 28 length

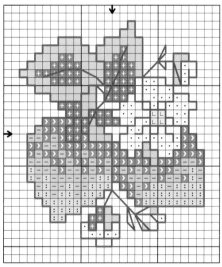

jar cover
Stitch Count: 26 width x 29 length

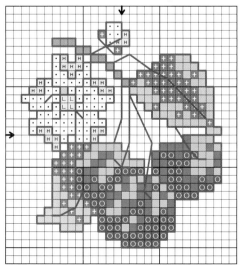

Sugar 'n Spice jar cover (as shown on page 60)
Stitch Count: 27 width x 26 length

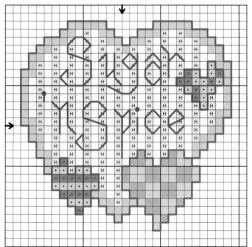

jar cover
Stitch Count: 29 width x 26 length

jar cover
Stitch Count: 25 width x 26 length

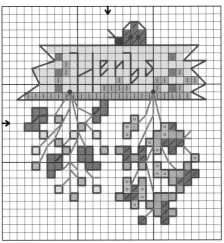

Fruit jar cover (as shown on page 60)
Stitch Count: 28 width x 29 length

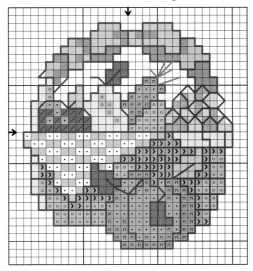

jar cover
Stitch Count: 27 width x 26 length

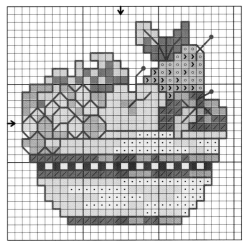

coaster
Stitch Count: 35 width x 33 length

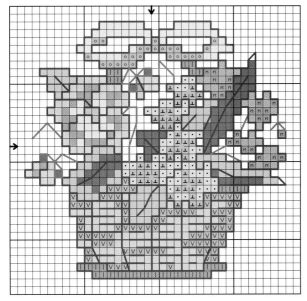

coaster
Stitch Count: 33 width x 34 length

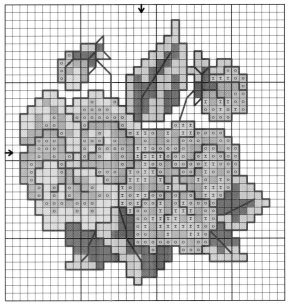

coaster
Stitch Count: 42 width x 42 length

DMC Floss

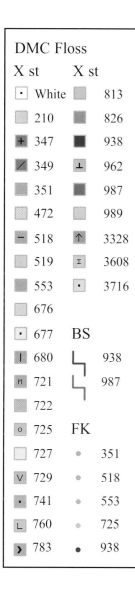

X st		X st	
·	White		813
	210		826
+	347		938
/	349	⊥	962
	351		987
	472		989
−	518	↑	3328
	519	I	3608
	553	·	3716
	676		
·	677	**BS**	
I	680		938
n	721		987
	722		
o	725	**FK**	
	727	•	351
V	729	•	518
·	741	•	553
L	760	•	725
❯	783	•	938

coaster
Stitch Count: 41 width x 40 length

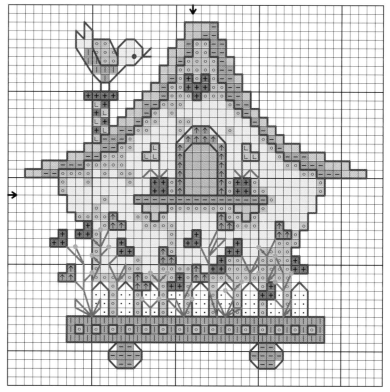

Fruit & Heart jar cover (as shown on page 67)
Stitch Count: 22 width x 27 length

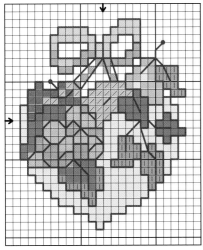

Geranium jar cover (as shown on page 67)
Stitch Count: 25 width x 28 length

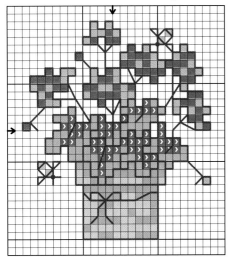

coaster
Stitch Count: 35 width x 33 length

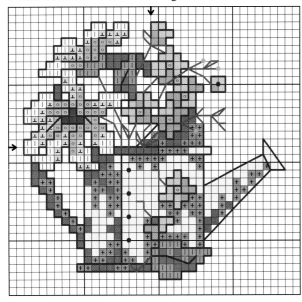

coaster
Stitch Count: 43 width x 45 length

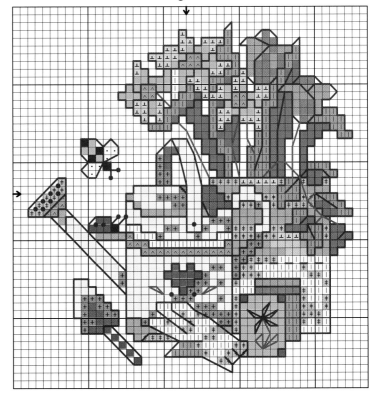

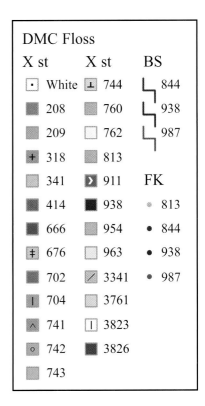

DMC Floss		
X st	X st	BS
· White	⊥ 744	844
208	760	938
209	762	987
+ 318	813	
341	▶ 911	FK
414	938	· 813
666	954	• 844
∓ 676	963	• 938
702	⁄ 3341	• 987
I 704	3761	
∧ 741	I 3823	
○ 742	3826	
743		

coaster
Stitch Count: 31 width x 33 length

coaster
Stitch Count: 40 width x 47 length

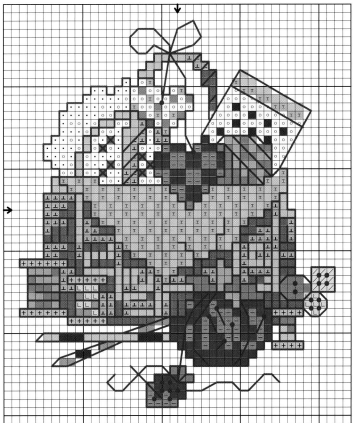

Harvest jar cover (as shown on page 67)
Stitch Count: 27 width x 29 length

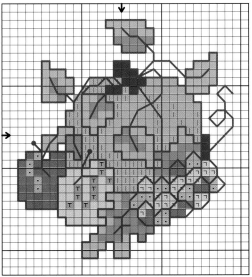

jar cover
Stitch Count: 28 width x 27 length

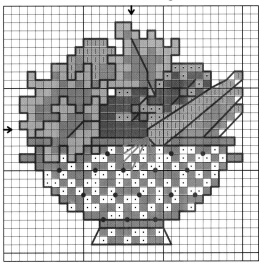

Cherry Pie jar cover (as shown on page 61)
Stitch Count: 27 width x 28 length

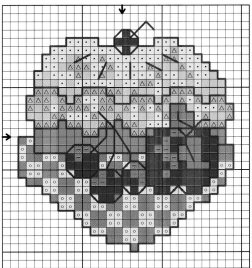

coaster
Stitch Count: 35 width x 33 length

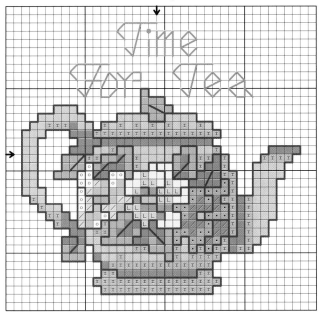

jar cover
Stitch Count: 22 width x 26 length

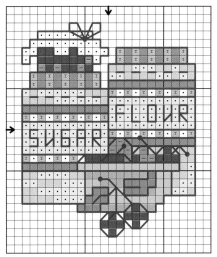

jar cover
Stitch Count: 27 width x 29 length

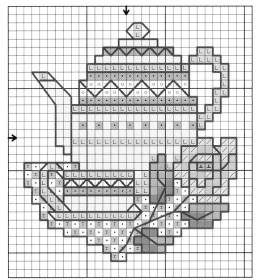

Shaker Shelf jar cover (as shown on page 61)
Stitch Count: 28 width x 26 length

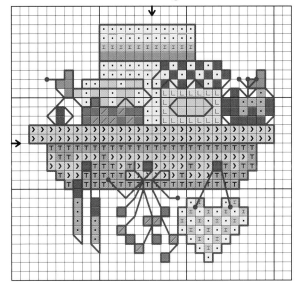

DMC Floss					
X st		**X st**		**BS**	
·	White	❯	738	⌐	702
╱	208	■	741	⌐	826
·	209	·	743	⌐	938
	318	╱	744		
⌐	341	−	762	**FK**	
−	350	I	813	●	702
·	351	■	817	●	938
+	402		818		
■	420	■	826		
T	436	·	827		
	472	■	938		
	676		958		
·	677		961		
	702	L	3716		
	704	■	3746		
	720	○	3823		
I	721	△	3827		
⊥	729				

coaster
Stitch Count: 35 width x 35 length

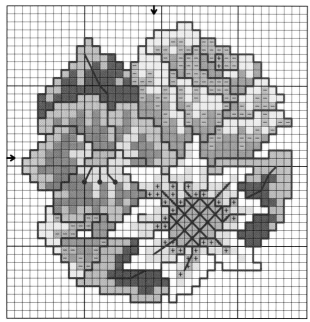

coaster
Stitch Count: 35 width x 33 length

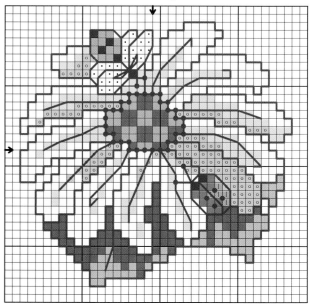

coaster
Stitch Count: 42 width x 42 length

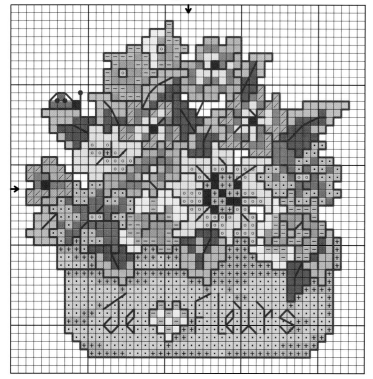

DMC Floss		
X st	X st	X st
⊡ White	⊙ 743	3776
208	744	▮ 3801
╱ 209	813	☐ 3823
210	826	
349	938	BS
⊡ 352	961	└ 938
400	━ 962	
⊡ 676	963	FK
✚ 729	987	● 938
742	989	

coaster
Stitch Count: 36 width x 30 length

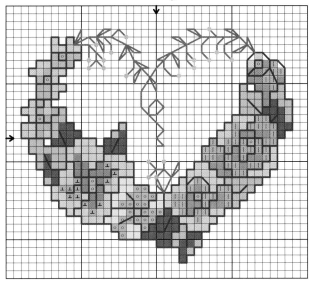

coaster
Stitch Count: 32 width x 32 length

coaster
Stitch Count: 32 width x 33 length

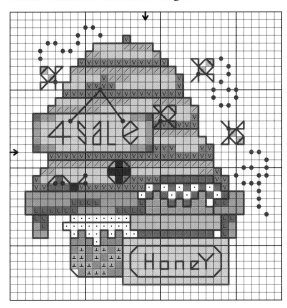

coaster
Stitch Count: 32 width x 34 length

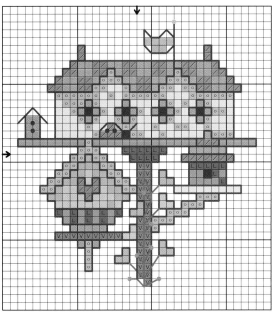

DMC Floss					
X st	X st	X st	X st	BS	FK
· White	676	813	987	700	209
208	L 700	+ 817	989	938	350
⊥ 209	703	825	☐ 3716	987	725
211	721	827	— 3820		813
349	○ 725	938	V 3829		825
╱ 350	727	961			938
351	╱ 729	I 962			962
					3820

coaster
Stitch Count: 41 width x 41 length

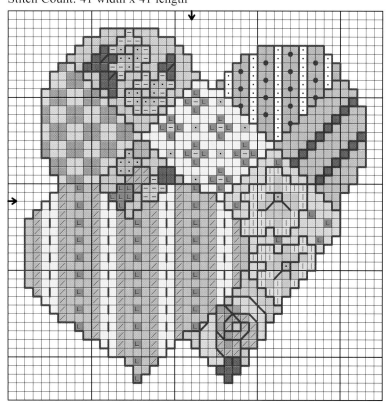

jar cover
Stitch Count: 27 width x 25 length

coaster
Stitch Count: 45 width x 39 length

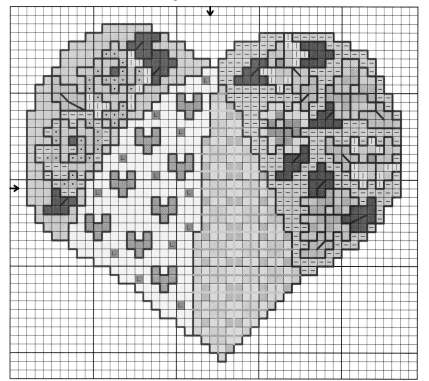

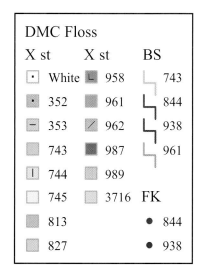

DMC Floss		
X st	X st	BS
· White	L 958	⌐ 743
▪ 352	961	⌐ 844
− 353	⁄ 962	⌐ 938
743	987	⌐ 961
I 744	989	
745	3716	FK
813		● 844
827		● 938

72

coaster
Stitch Count: 45 width x 42 length

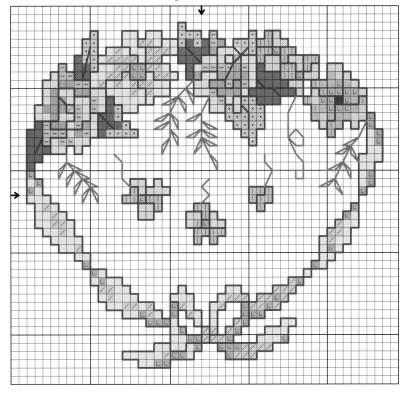

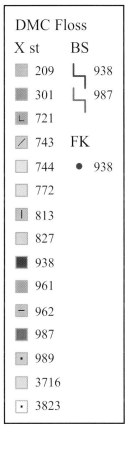

DMC Floss

X st		BS	
▨	209	⌐	938
▩	301	⌐	987
L	721		
╱	743	FK	
▨	744	●	938
▨	772		
I	813		
▨	827		
■	938		
▨	961		
−	962		
▨	987		
·	989		
▨	3716		
·	3823		

coaster
Stitch Count: 48 width x 49 length

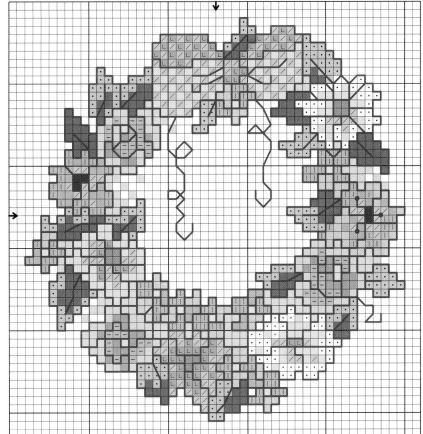

Designs for Mugs

Pagoda mug (as shown on page 74)
Stitch Count: 59 width x 42 length

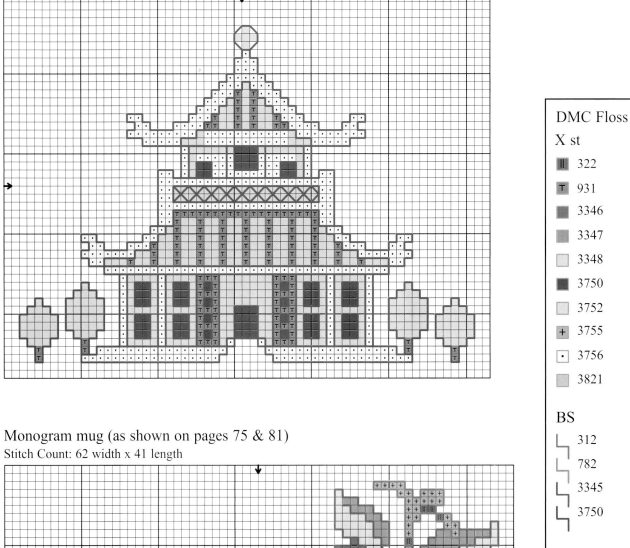

Monogram mug (as shown on pages 75 & 81)
Stitch Count: 62 width x 41 length

DMC Floss

X st

‖	322
T	931
■	3346
■	3347
▫	3348
■	3750
▫	3752
+	3755
·	3756
▫	3821

BS

└	312
└	782
└	3345
└	3750

BS 2-strands

└	322

FK

●	3821

Stitch Count: 52 width x 45 length

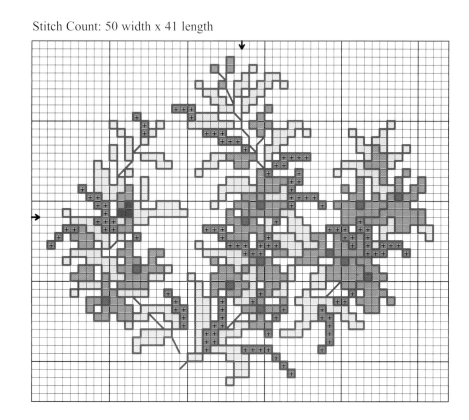

DMC Floss

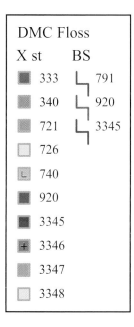

X st		BS	
■	333	⌐	791
■	340	⌐	920
■	721	⌐	3345
□	726		
L	740		
■	920		
■	3345		
+	3346		
■	3347		
□	3348		

Stitch Count: 50 width x 41 length

Stitch Count: 54 width x 45 length

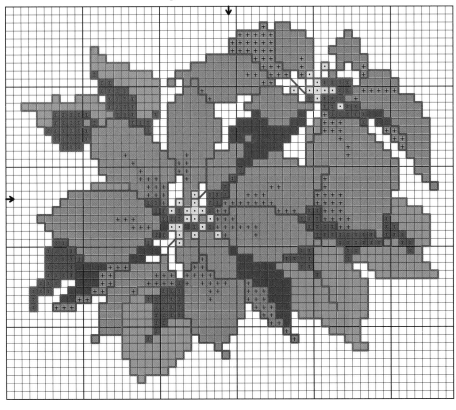

Stitch Count: 49 width x 45 length

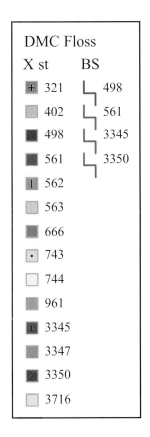

DMC Floss

X st		BS	
+	321	⌐	498
	402	⌐	561
	498	⌐	3345
	561	⌐	3350
	562		
	563		
	666		
·	743		
	744		
	961		
+	3345		
	3347		
	3350		
	3716		

Stitch Count: 59 width x 46 length

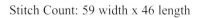

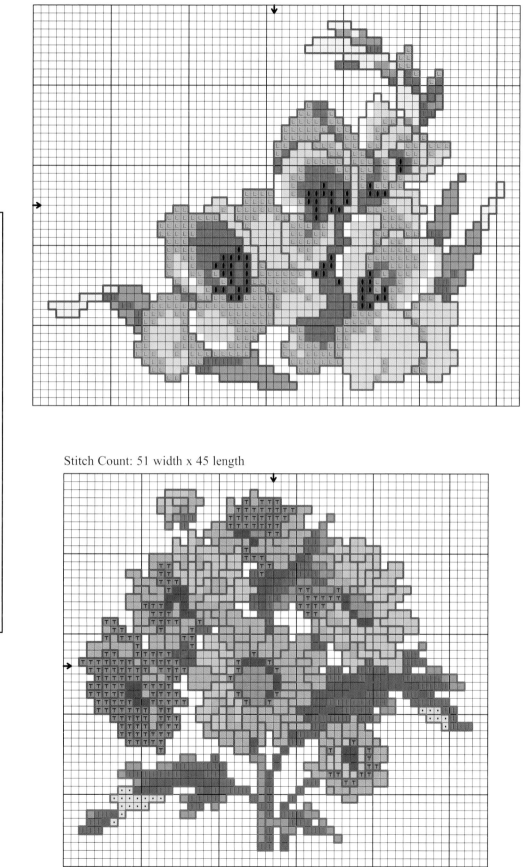

DMC Floss

X st		BS	
■	350	⌐	433
L	352	⌐	817
■	433	⌐	3345
■	435		
▨	444		
▨	741		
□	746		
▨	754		
□	772		
▣	817		
T	900		
▨	3345		
I	3346		
▨	3347		
·	3348		

Stitch Count: 51 width x 45 length

When's Lunch? mug (as shown on page 75)
Stitch Count: 44 width x 42 length

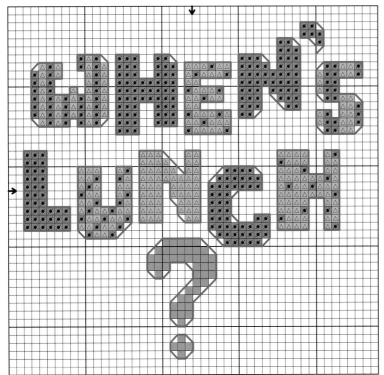

Peace and Plenty mug (as shown on pages 74 & 81)
Stitch Count: 57 width x 44 length

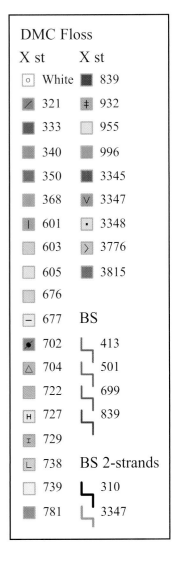

DMC Floss

X st		X st	
○	White	■	839
╱	321	‡	932
■	333		955
	340		996
	350	■	3345
	368	V	3347
I	601	·	3348
	603	⟩	3776
	605		3815
	676		
−	677	**BS**	
●	702	⌐	413
△	704	⌐	501
	722	⌐	699
H	727	⌐	839
I	729		
L	738	**BS 2-strands**	
	739	⌐	310
	781	⌐	3347

MOM mug (as shown on page 81)
Stitch Count: 80 width x 24 length

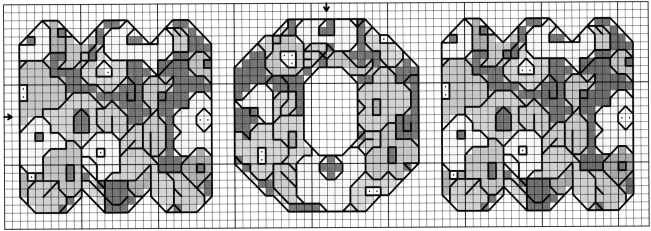

Stitch Count: 66 width x 24 length

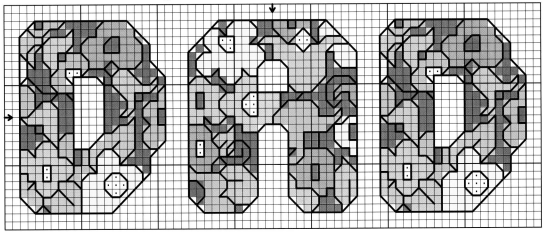

DMC Floss

X st

·	White
■	367
▦	553
■	666
▨	742
□	745
▨	809
▨	989
▨	3608

BS

└ 310

Stitch Count: 35 width x 23 length

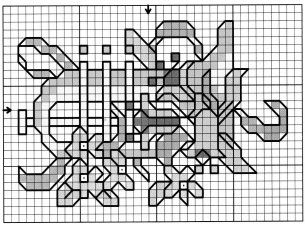

Stitch Count: 52 width x 44 length

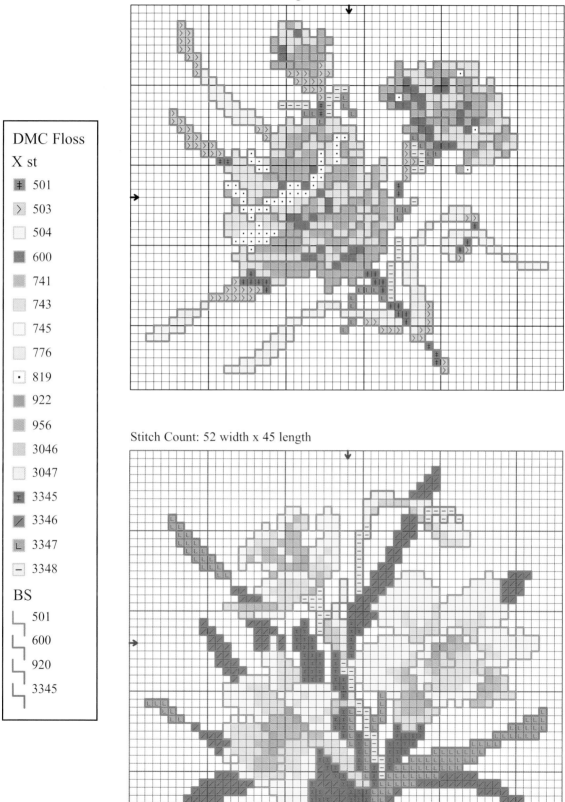

DMC Floss
X st

‡	501
>	503
	504
▨	600
	741
	743
	745
	776
·	819
	922
	956
	3046
	3047
ꞱI	3345
◢	3346
L	3347
–	3348

BS

⌐	501
⌐	600
⌐	920
⌐	3345

Stitch Count: 52 width x 45 length

Teacups mug (as shown on page 75)
Stitch Count: 36 width x 41 length

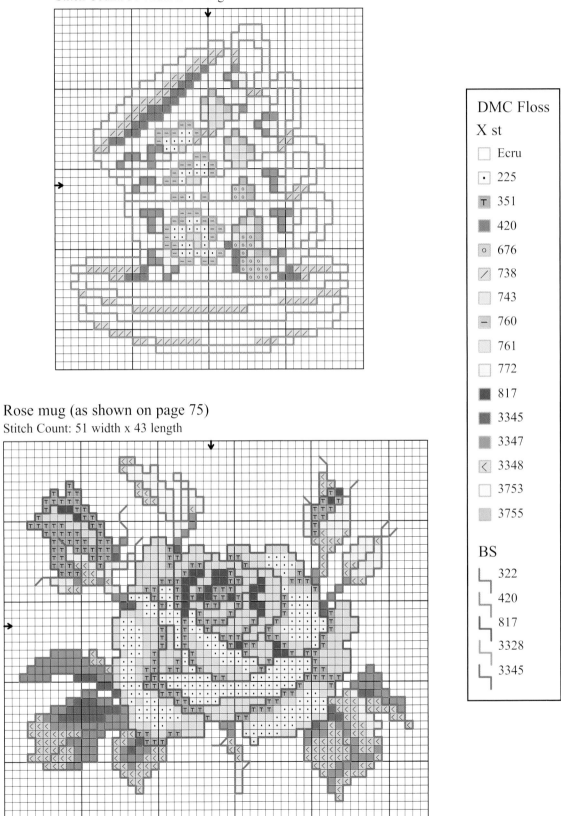

Rose mug (as shown on page 75)
Stitch Count: 51 width x 43 length

DMC Floss

X st

☐ Ecru
· 225
T 351
■ 420
○ 676
╱ 738
☐ 743
— 760
☐ 761
☐ 772
■ 817
■ 3345
■ 3347
< 3348
☐ 3753
■ 3755

BS

322
420
817
3328
3345

Stitch Count: 49 width x 45 length

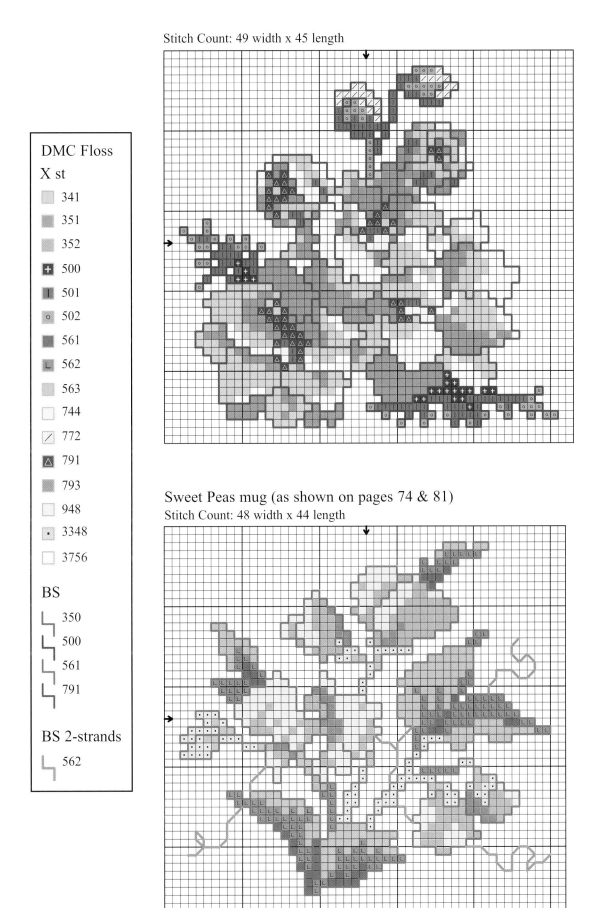

DMC Floss
X st

	341
	351
	352
+	500
I	501
o	502
	561
L	562
	563
	744
/	772
△	791
	793
	948
·	3348
	3756

BS

⌐	350
⌐	500
⌐	561
⌐	791

BS 2-strands

⌐	562

Sweet Peas mug (as shown on pages 74 & 81)
Stitch Count: 48 width x 44 length

Designs for Small Acessories

small magnet
Stitch Count: 25 width x 25 length

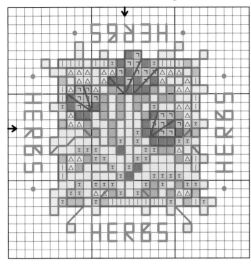

Radishes small magnet (as shown on page 87)
Stitch Count: 24 width x 25 length

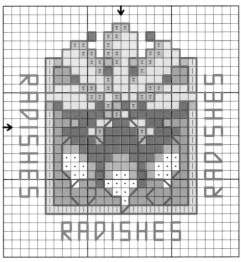

small magnet
Stitch Count: 24 width x 24 length

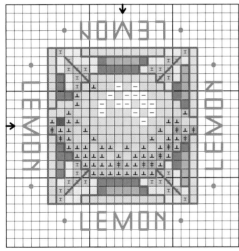

small magnet
Stitch Count: 24 width x 26 length

small magnet
Stitch Count: 24 width x 24 length

small magnet
Stitch Count: 24 width x 24 length

Watermelon small magnet (as shown on page 87)
Stitch Count: 24 width x 25 length

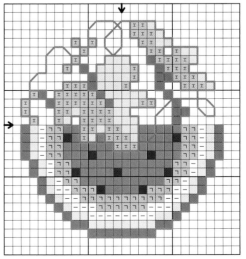

King keychain (as shown on page 87)
Stitch Count: 22 width x 25 length

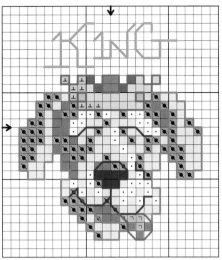

Queen keychain (as shown on page 87)
Stitch Count: 23 width x 25 length

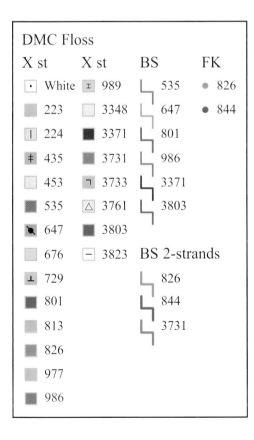

Bunny pencil topper (as shown on page 95)
Stitch Count: 25 width x 24 length

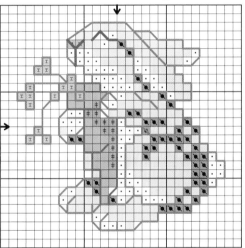

Mouse small magnet (as shown on page 86)
Stitch Count: 24 width x 25 length

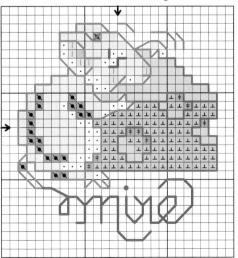

DMC Floss			
X st	X st	BS	FK
· White	I 989	└ 535	● 826
▨ 223	▨ 3348	└ 647	● 844
I 224	■ 3371	└ 801	
‡ 435	▨ 3731	└ 986	
▨ 453	˥ 3733	└ 3371	
▨ 535	△ 3761	└ 3803	
◣ 647	▨ 3803		
▨ 676	− 3823	BS 2-strands	
⊥ 729		└ 826	
■ 801		└ 844	
▨ 813		└ 3731	
▨ 826			
▨ 977			
▨ 986			

small magnet
Stitch Count: 23 width x 25 length

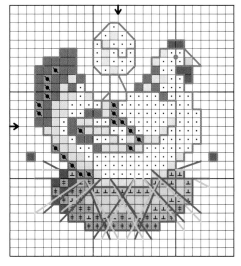

small magnet
Stitch Count: 22 width x 24 length

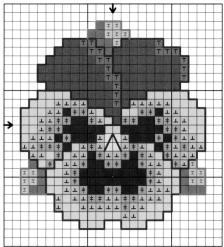

Bird keychain (as shown on page 87)
Stitch Count: 26 width x 26 length

small magnet
Stitch Count: 25 width x 24 length

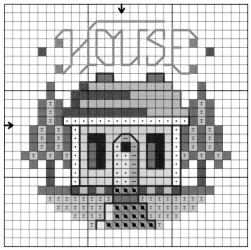

small magnet
Stitch Count: 26 width x 24 length

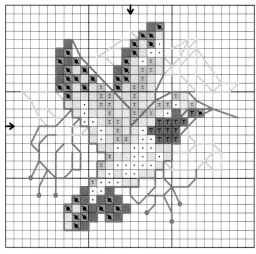

Beehive pencil topper (as shown on page 95)
Stitch Count: 26 width x 26 length

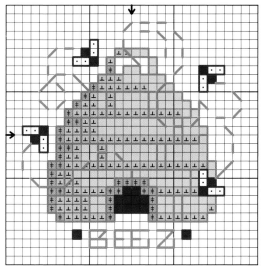

Sun keychain (as shown on page 86)
Stitch Count: 27 width x 26 length

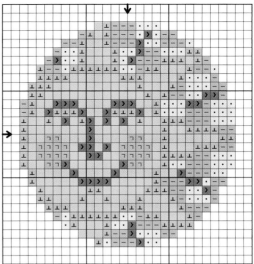

small magnet
Stitch Count: 27 width x 25 length

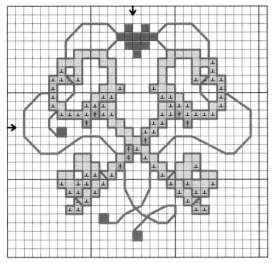

small magnet
Stitch Count: 26 width x 26 length

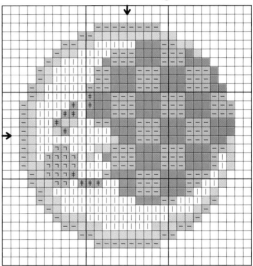

small magnet
Stitch Count: 27 width x 27 length

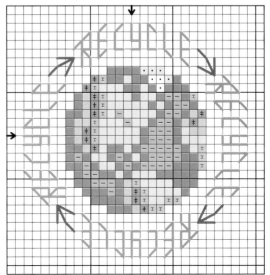

DMC Floss			
X st	X st	BS	BS 2-strands
· White	826	434	304
223	986	435	826
304	I 989	535	
❯ 434	3348	729	FK
‡ 435	3371	801	● 535
453	T 3731	986	● 3371
535	˥ 3733	989	● 3731
● 647	· 3761	3371	
676	3803	3731	
⊥ 729	I 3823	3803	
801			
– 813			

Teacher pencil topper (as shown on page 95)
Stitch Count: 24 width x 26 length

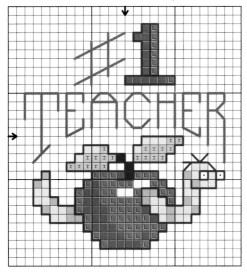

Water Me pencil topper (as shown on page 95)
Stitch Count: 27 width x 25 length

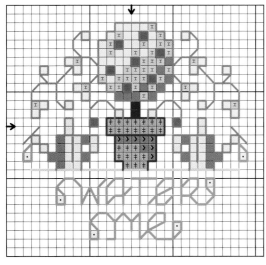

Grocery List small magnet (as shown on page 87)
Stitch Count: 26 width x 25 length

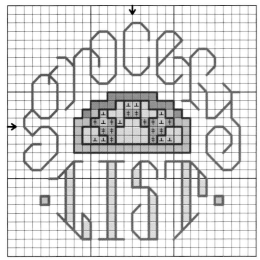

Pencil small magnet (as shown on page 87)
Stitch Count: 27 width x 21 length

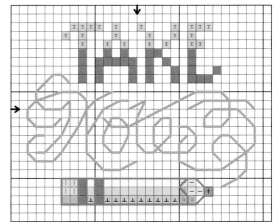

small magnet
Stitch Count: 27 width x 26 length

small magnet
Stitch Count: 24 width x 24 length

small magnet
Stitch Count: 26 width x 24 length

1st Place small magnet
(as shown on page 87)
Stitch Count: 20 width x 23 length

small magnet
Stitch Count: 24 width x 24 length

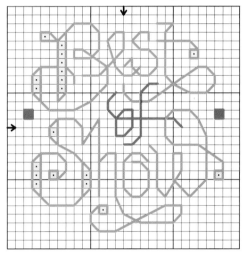

small magnet
Stitch Count: 30 width x 27 length

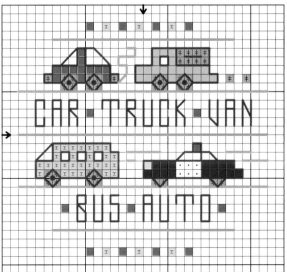

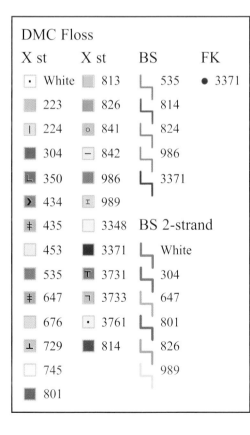

DMC Floss			
X st	X st	BS	FK
· White	813	⌐ 535	● 3371
223	826	⌐ 814	
Ι 224	○ 841	⌐ 824	
304	− 842	⌐ 986	
∟ 350	986	⌐ 3371	
❯ 434	Ι 989		
‡ 435	3348	BS 2-strand	
453	3371	⌐ White	
535	Τ 3731	⌐ 304	
‡ 647	⌐ 3733	⌐ 647	
676	· 3761	⌐ 801	
⊥ 729	814	⌐ 826	
745		⌐ 989	
801			

93

small magnet
Stitch Count: 24 width x 22 length

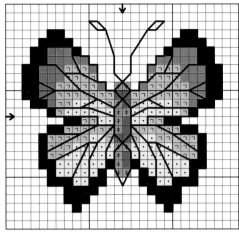

magnet
Stitch Count: 30 width x 22 length

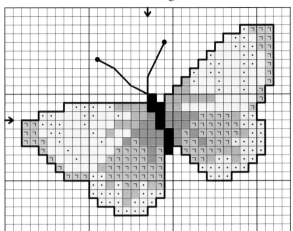

small magnet
Stitch Count: 24 width x 24 length

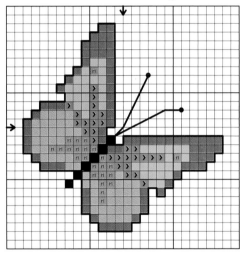

DMC Floss		
X st		**X st**
o	309	3705
■	310	/ 3706
	400	˥ 3766
	598	3799
‡	647	› 3810
–	676	· 3811
	744	ᴨ 3826
	783	
	806	**BS**
	815	⌐ 310
I	899	
T	958	**FK**
I	959	• 310

small magnet
Stitch Count: 16 width x 17 length

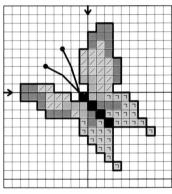

small magnet
Stitch Count: 20 width x 20 length

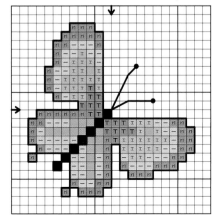

small magnet
Stitch Count: 13 width x 15 length

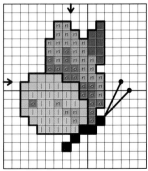

small magnet
Stitch Count: 13 width x 13 length

magnet
Stitch Count: 25 width x 29 length

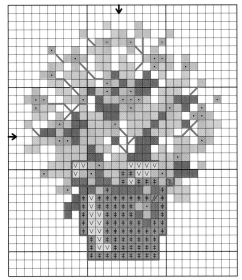

magnet
Stitch Count: 26 width x 29 length

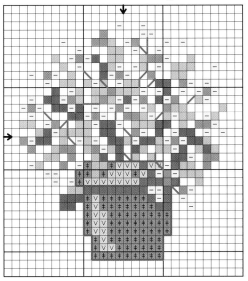

magnet
Stitch Count: 28 width x 23 length

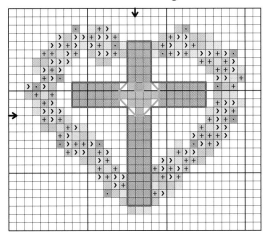

small magnet
Stitch Count: 27 width x 24 length

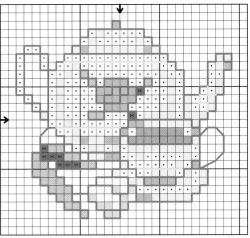

Pansy luggage tag (as shown on page 95)
Stitch Count: 29 width x 29 length

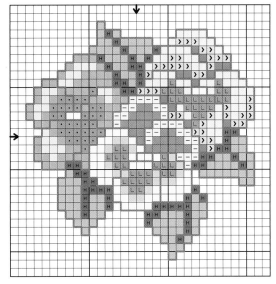

Humming Bird magnet (as shown on page 86)
Stitch Count: 28 width x 30 length

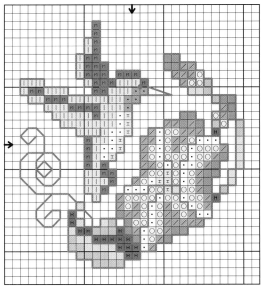

Flower Basket key ring (as shown on page 86)
Stitch Count: 26 width x 34 length

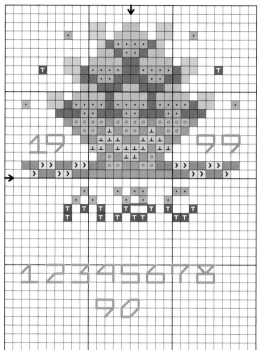

luggage tag
Stitch Count: 24 width x 28 length

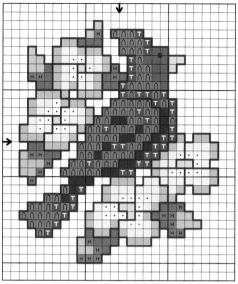

magnet
Stitch Count: 28 width x 27 length

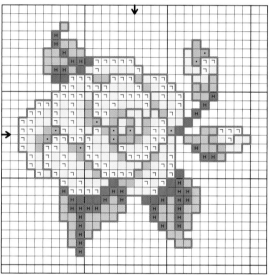

Floral Heart magnet (as shown on page 87)
Stitch Count: 27 width x 25 length

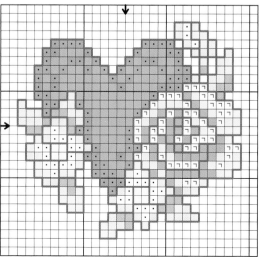

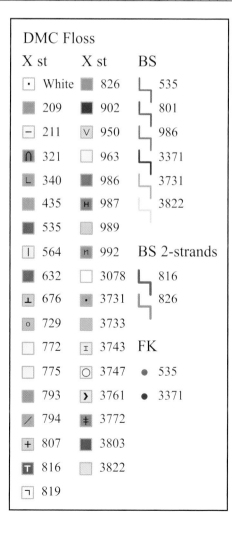

DMC Floss

X st		X st		BS	
·	White		826		535
	209		902		801
−	211	V	950		986
∩	321		963		3371
L	340	H	987		3731
	435		989		3822
	535	n	992		
I	564				**BS 2-strands**
	632		3078		816
⊥	676	·	3731		826
o	729		3733		
	772	I	3743		**FK**
	775	O	3747	●	535
	793	❭	3761	●	3371
/	794	‡	3772		
+	807		3803		
T	816		3822		
┐	819				

small magnet
Stitch Count: 24 width x 24 length

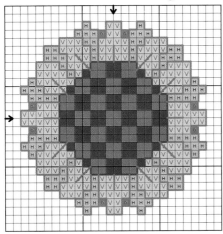

magnet
Stitch Count: 26 width x 27 length

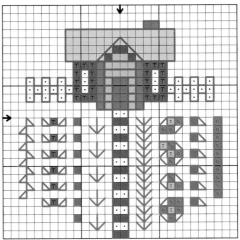

Chilies magnet (as shown on page 87)
Stitch Count: 29 width x 30 length

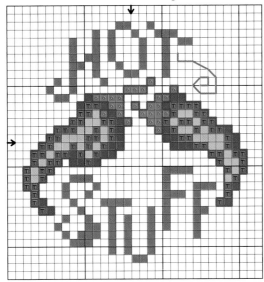

magnet
Stitch Count: 25 width x 29 length

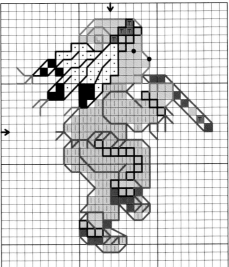

Chocolates magnet (as shown on page 86)
Stitch Count: 30 width x 30 length

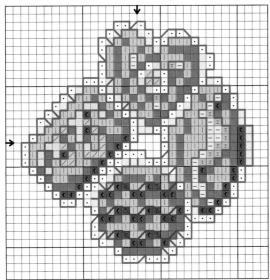

Mrs. Mouse magnet (as shown on page 86)
Stitch Count: 32 width x 32 length

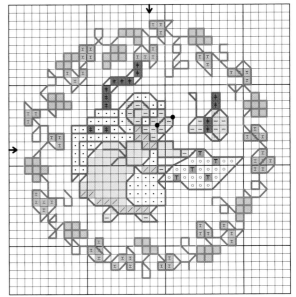

Noah's Ark luggage tag (as shown on page 95)
Stitch Count: 30 width x 30 length

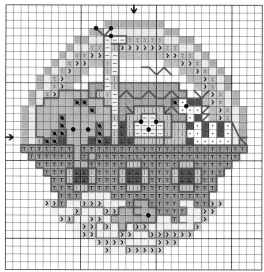

Sailboat luggage tag (as shown on page 95)
Stitch Count: 30 width x 30 length

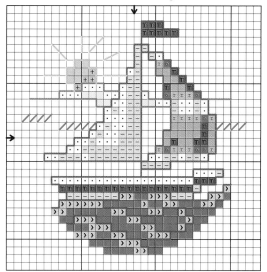

luggage tag
Stitch Count: 29 width x 29 length

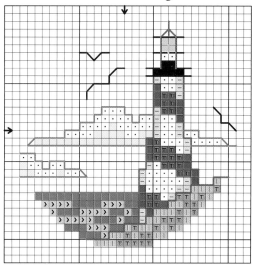

Sports luggage tag (as shown on page 95)
Stitch Count: 30 width x 30 length

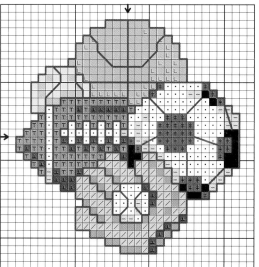

DMC Floss

X st		X st		X st		BS	
·	White	V	676	·	819		208
	210		704		841		310
■	310		726	/	842		322
	322		727	o	911		434
	351	H	729	■	938		561
	402	−	739	I	954		742
‡	413	+	742	>	3325		817
−	415	o	762	/	3688		938
⌐	433	−	772	L	3776		3799
	434		775	■	3799		
T	435		776			**FK**	
I	437	◀	801			●	310
	561		807				
◣	646		815				
	648	T	817				

Designs for Bookmarks

Best friends grow together with love!

Feather bookmark (as shown on page 101)
Stitch Count: 24 width x 93 length

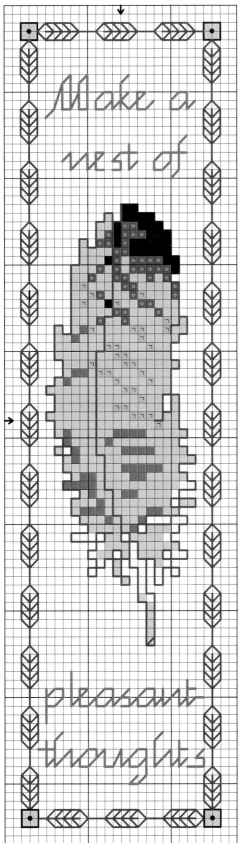

Fishing bookmark (as shown on page 100)
Stitch Count: 26 width x 96 length

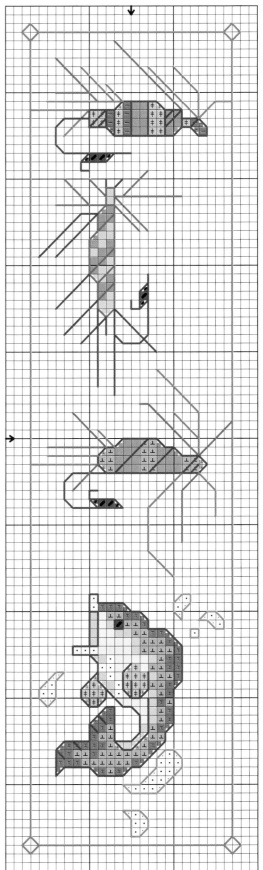

Stitch Count: 27 width x 65 length

Stitch Count: 30 width x 69 length

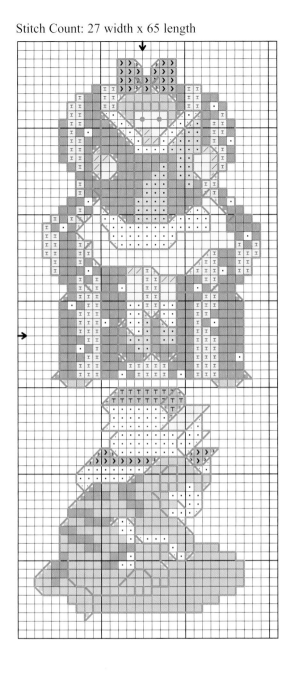

DMC Floss

X st		X st		X st		X st		X st		BS		BS		FK	
·	White	T	434		772		958	I	3815		310		3790	●	310
■	310		436		775	›	959	⊥	3817		317		3799	●	317
-	349	o	645		794		3078		3822		349		3815		
	351	⌐	648		841	T	3341				434				
	400		676	·	842		3608				826	BS 2-strands			
◪	413	‡	738	/	945	I	3747				3021		400		
I	415		761		951	I	3776								

Stitch Count: 26 width x 96 length

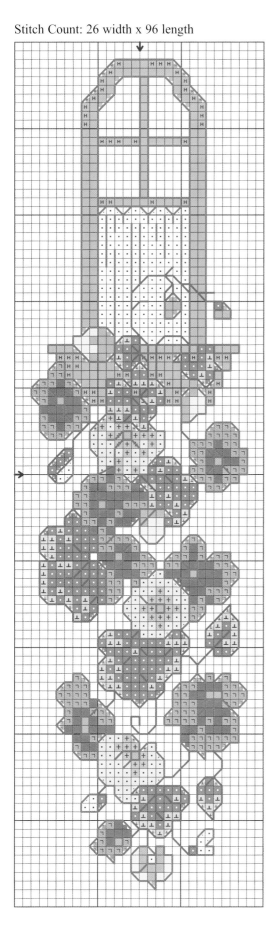

Birdhouse bookmark (as shown on page 101)
Stitch Count: 28 width x 98 length

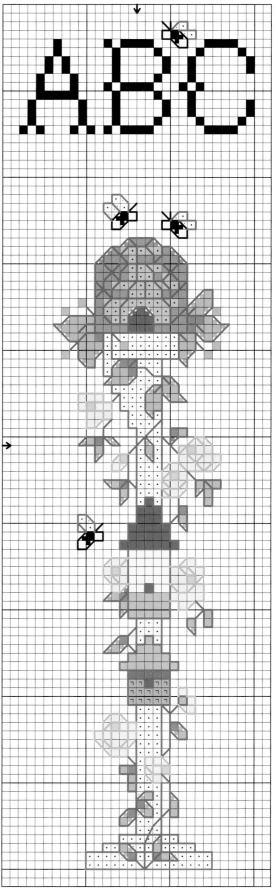

Topiary bookmark (as shown on page 101)
Stitch Count: 24 width x 61 length

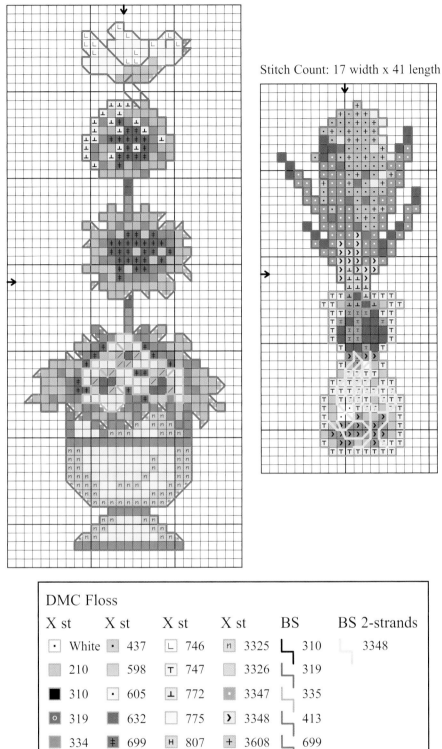

Stitch Count: 17 width x 41 length

Butterfly bookmark
(as shown on page 109)
Stitch Count: 21 width x 80 length

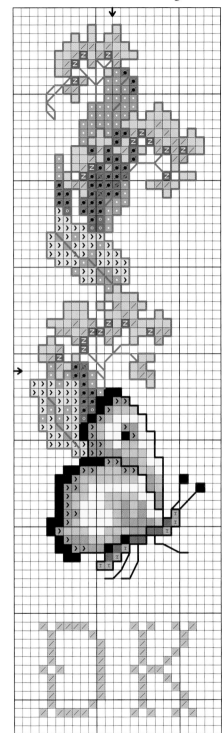

DMC Floss

X st		X st		X st		X st		BS		BS 2-strands	
·	White	·	437	L	746	n	3325	⌐	310		3348
	210		598	T	747		3326	⌐	319		
■	310	·	605	⊥	772	·	3347	⌐	335		
o	319		632		775	⟩	3348	⌐	413		
	334	‡	699	H	807	+	3608	⌐	699		
/	335		702	Z	816	⊥	3778	⌐	816		
	350		704		818		38268	⌐	915		
⌐	352	·	718	I	841			⌐	975		
	413		722		915			⌐	986		
⟩	414		725		986						
	435		745	●	987						

Stitch Count: 27 width x 90 length

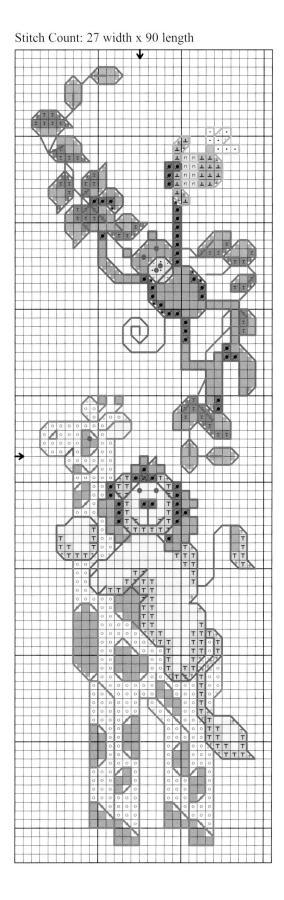

Stitch Count: 28 width x 89 length

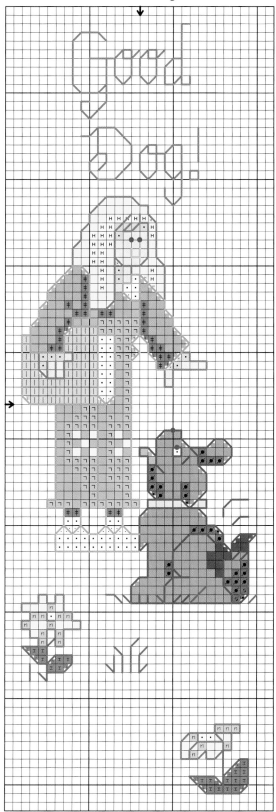

Stitch Count: 28 width x 56 length

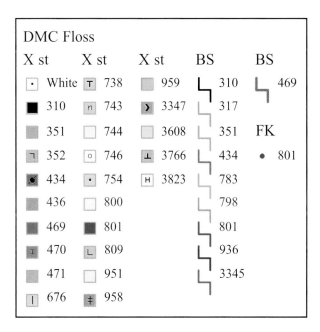

Stitch Count: 26 width x 61 length

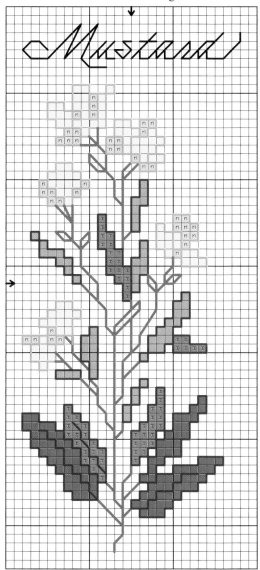

DMC Floss				
X st	X st	X st	BS	BS
· White	T 738	959	310	469
■ 310	n 743	› 3347	317	
351	744	3608	351	FK
⌐ 352	○ 746	⊥ 3766	434	• 801
◉ 434	· 754	H 3823	783	
436	800		798	
469	■ 801		801	
⊥ 470	L 809		936	
471	951		3345	
I 676	‡ 958			

107

Stitch Count: 26 width x 55 length

Stitch Count: 27 width x 57 length

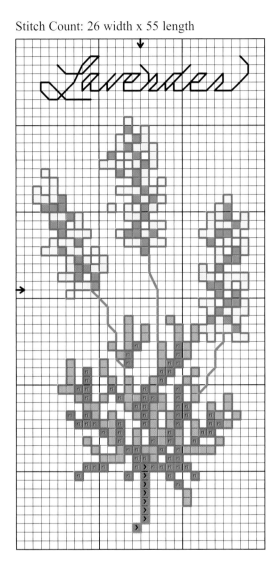

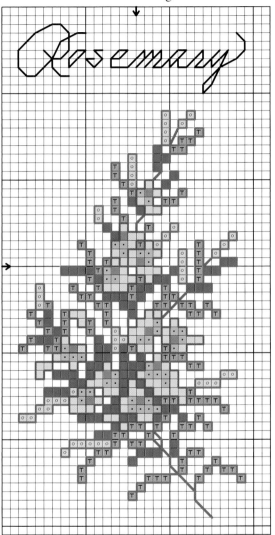

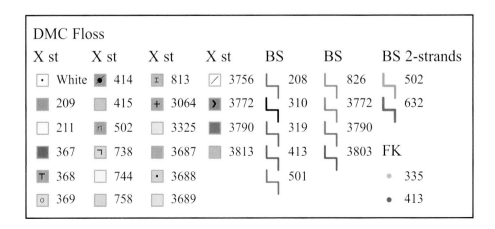

DMC Floss

X st		X st		X st		X st		BS		BS		BS 2-strands	
·	White	●	414	I	813	/	3756	⌐	208	⌐	826	⌐	502
	209		415	+	3064	❯	3772	⌐	310	⌐	3772	⌐	632
	211	n	502		3325		3790	⌐	319	⌐	3790		
	367	⌐	738		3687		3813	⌐	413	⌐	3803	FK	
T	368		744	·	3688			⌐	501			●	335
o	369		758		3689							●	413

108

Stitch Count: 28 width x 95 length

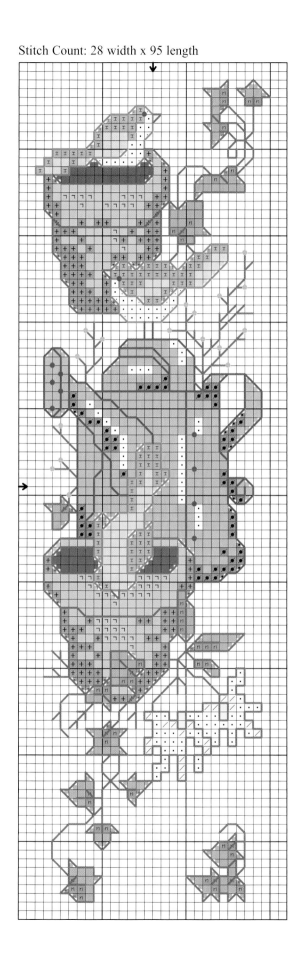

109

Dove & Heart bookmark (as shown on page 109)
Stitch Count: 28 width x 73 length

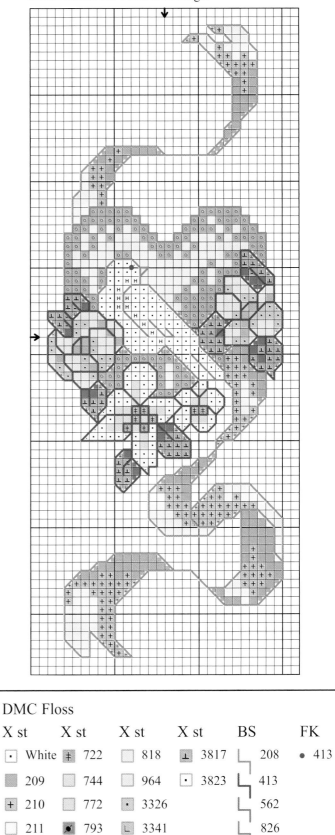

Baker's Rack bookmark
(as shown on page 101)
Stitch Count: 24 width x 79 length

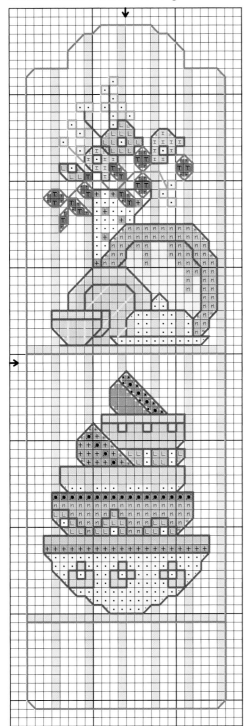

DMC Floss					
X st	X st	X st	X st	BS	FK
· White	‡ 722	818	⊥ 3817	⌐ 208	● 413
209	744	964	· 3823	⌐ 413	
+ 210	772	· 3326		⌐ 562	
211	● 793	L 3341		⌐ 826	
335	794	n 3753		⌐ 841	
T 562	800	H 3756		964	
I 605	o 813	3815			

Best Friends bookmark
(as shown on page 100)
Stitch Count: 25 width x 89 length

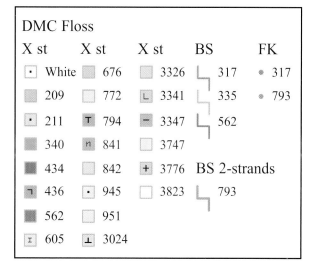

DMC Floss				
X st	X st	X st	BS	FK
· White	676	3326	⌐ 317	● 317
209	772	∟ 3341	⌐ 335	● 793
· 211	⊤ 794	− 3347	⌐ 562	
340	�-n 841	3747		
434	842	+ 3776	BS 2-strands	
⌐ 436	· 945	3823	⌐ 793	
562	951			
I 605	⊥ 3024			

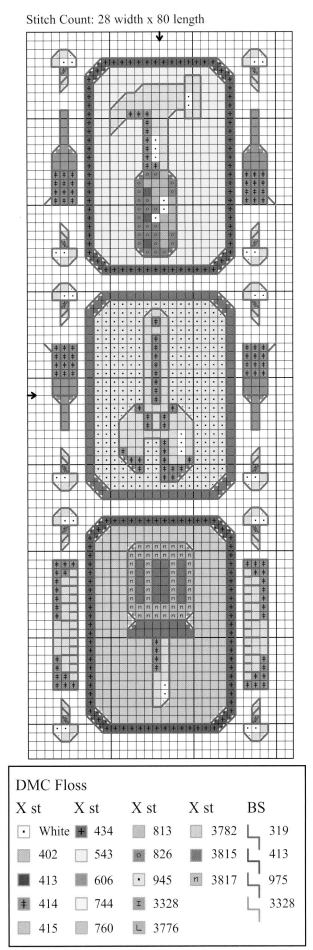

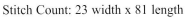

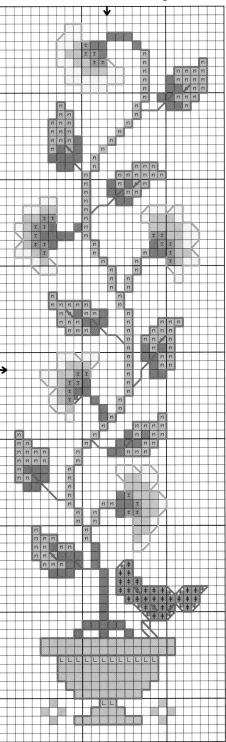

DMC Floss

X st		X st		X st		X st		BS	
·	White	+	434		813		3782	⌐	319
	402		543	o	826		3815	⌐	413
	413		606	·	945	n	3817	⌐	975
+	414		744	I	3328			⌐	3328
	415		760	L	3776				

Birds bookmark (as shown on page 100)
Stitch Count: 27 width x 79 length

Stitch Count: 27 width x 78 length

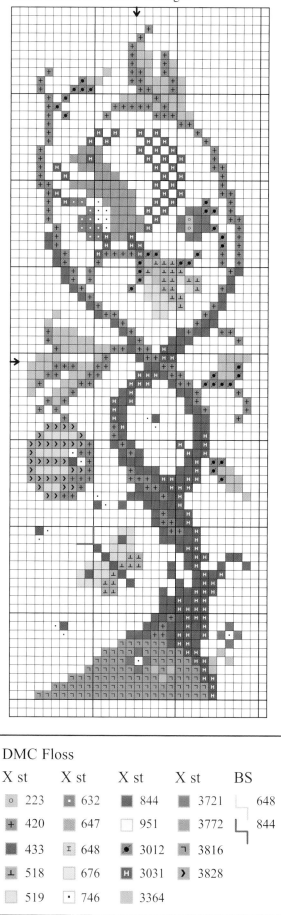

DMC Floss				
X st	X st	X st	X st	BS
○ 223	⊡ 632	■ 844	■ 3721	⌐ 648
+ 420	▦ 647	☐ 951	▦ 3772	⌐ 844
■ 433	ⅈ 648	● 3012	⅂ 3816	
⊥ 518	▨ 676	Н 3031	› 3828	
▨ 519	· 746	▨ 3364		

113

Angel oval ornament (as shown on page 114)
Stitch Count: 26 width x 40 length

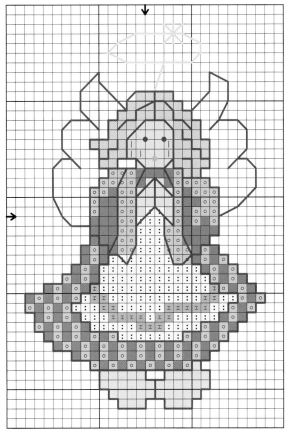

Stitch Count: 20 width x 20 length

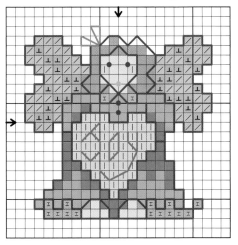

Stitch Count: 22 width x 21 length

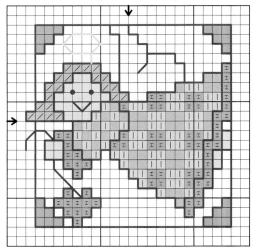

Stitch Count: 28 width x 38 length

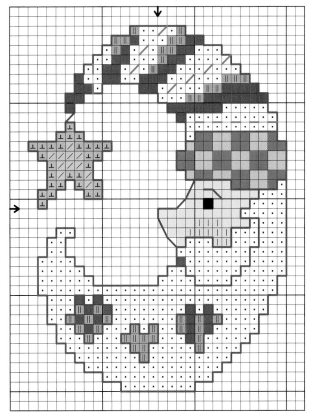

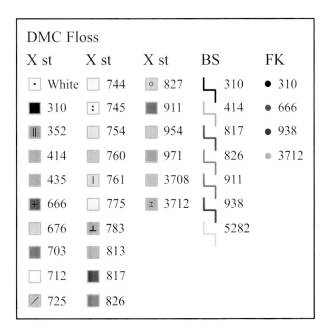

DMC Floss

X st		X st		X st		BS		FK	
⋅	White		744	o	827	⌐	310	●	310
■	310	:	745		911	⌐	414	●	666
‖	352		754		954	⌐	817	●	938
	414		760		971	⌐	826	●	3712
	435	I	761		3708	⌐	911		
+	666		775	I	3712	⌐	938		
	676	⊥	783			⌐	5282		
	703		813						
	712	■	817						
/	725		826						

NOEL octagonal ornament
(as shown on page 114)
Stitch Count: 21 width x 21 length

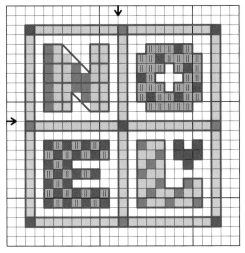

Santa Sign oval ornament
(as shown on page 115)
Stitch Count: 23 width x 41 length

Snowman oval ornament (as shown on page 115)
Stitch Count: 28 width x 37 length

Stitch Count: 28 width x 39 length

Angel stocking ornament (as shown on page 121)
Stitch Count: 38 width x 51 length

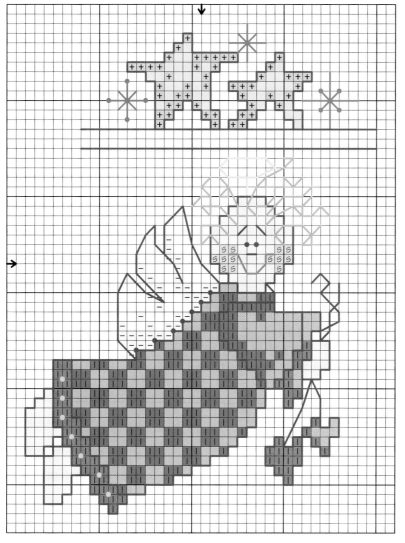

Stitch Count: 21 width x 21 length

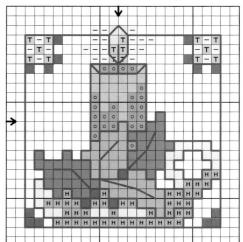

Stitch Count: 21 width x 21 length

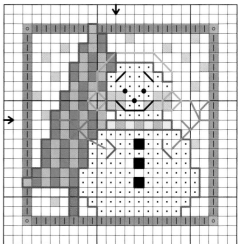

Stitch Count: 26 width x 26 length

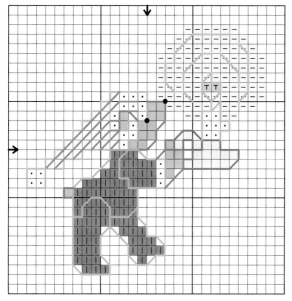

Hearts & Stars octagonal ornament
(as shown on page 115)
Stitch Count: 22 width x 21 length

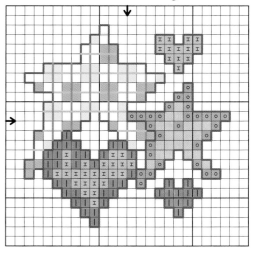

Santa snowflake ornament
(as shown on page 115)
Stitch Count: 19 width x 21 length

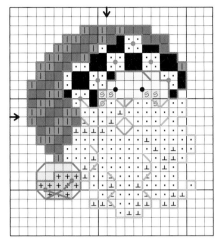

Stitch Count: 16 width x 22 length

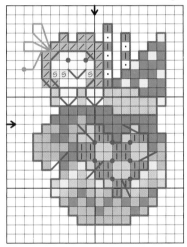

Santa Claus snowflake ornament
(as shown on page 121)
Stitch Count: 19 width x 27 length

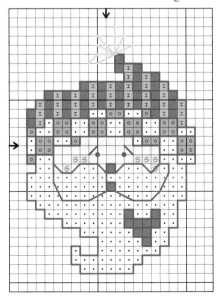

Teddy Bear stocking ornament (as shown on page 121)
Stitch Count: 41 width x 52 length

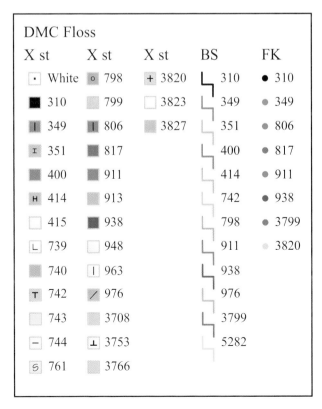

DMC Floss				
X st	X st	X st	BS	FK
· White	o 798	+ 3820	310	● 310
■ 310	799	3823	349	● 349
I 349	I 806	3827	351	● 806
I 351	817		400	● 817
400	911		414	● 911
H 414	913		742	● 938
415	938		798	● 3799
L 739	948		911	3820
740	I 963		938	
T 742	/ 976		976	
743	3708		3799	
- 744	⊥ 3753		5282	
S 761	3766			

119

Penguin stocking ornament (as shown on page 121)
Stitch Count: 42 width x 51 length

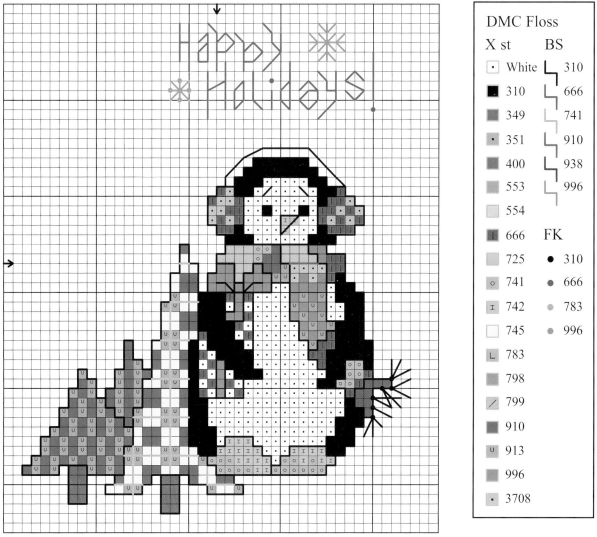

DMC Floss		
X st		BS
· White	⌐	310
■ 310	⌐	666
■ 349	⌐	741
· 351	⌐	910
■ 400	⌐	938
■ 553	⌐	996
554		
▌ 666	FK	
725	●	310
○ 741	●	666
I 742	●	783
745	●	996
L 783		
798		
╱ 799		
910		
U 913		
996		
· 3708		

Heart octagonal ornament (as shown on page 114)

Stitch Count: 27 width x 26 length

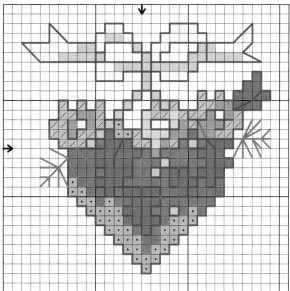

Stitch Count: 29 width x 25 length

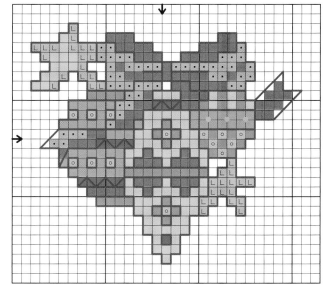

121

stocking ornament
Stitch Count: 48 width x 54 length

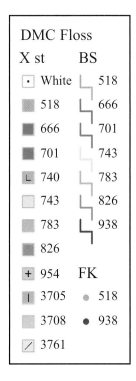

DMC Floss

X st		BS	
·	White	∟	518
▨	518	∟	666
■	666	∟	701
■	701	∟	743
∟	740	∟	783
▨	743	∟	826
▨	783	∟	938
■	826		
+	954	FK	
⌶	3705	○	518
▨	3708	●	938
⧄	3761		

Hearts, Stars & Candy heart ornament
(as shown on page 115)

Stitch Count: 29 width x 27 length

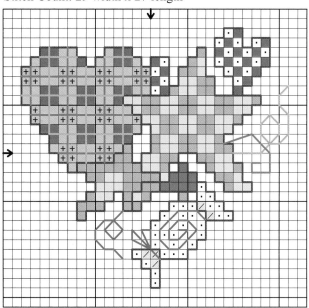

Stitch Count: 27 width x 26 length

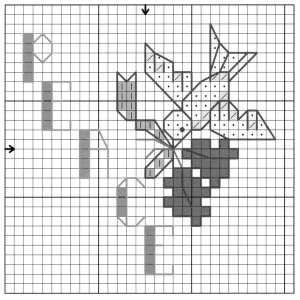

122

stocking ornament
Stitch Count: 40 width x 53 length

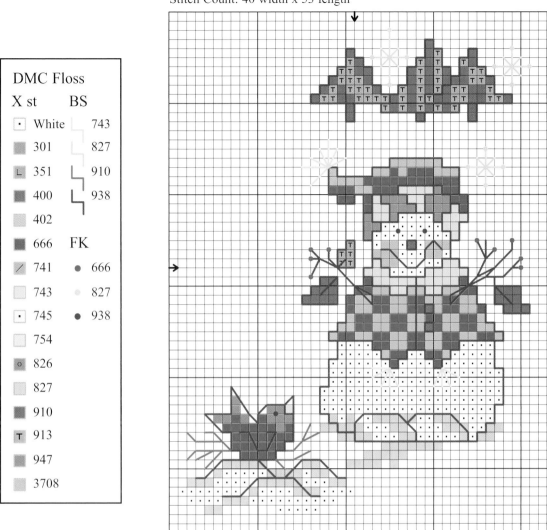

DMC Floss

X st		BS	
⊡	White		743
▨	301		827
L	351		910
▪	400		938
▨	402		
▪	666	FK	
╱	741	●	666
▫	743	●	827
·	745	●	938
▫	754		
o	826		
▫	827		
▨	910		
T	913		
▨	947		
▨	3708		

Candles heart ornament
(as shown on page 114)
Stitch Count: 24 width x 27 length

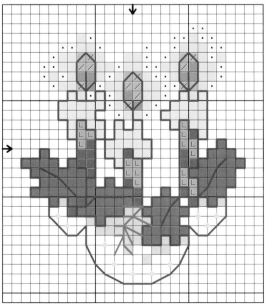

Stitch Count: 32 width x 29 length

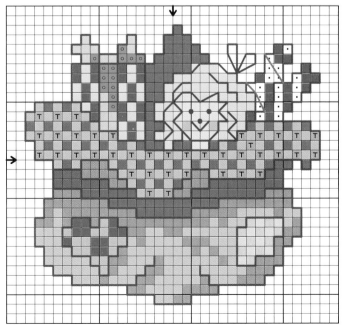

123

stocking ornament
Stitch Count: 41 width x 49 length

DMC Floss

X st		BS	
·	White	⌐	518
■	321	⌐	666
▨	353	⌐	783
▨	402	⌐	912
▨	518	⌐	938
○	519		
•	603	FK	
▨	605		
■	666	●	310
−	738	●	666
⁄	743	●	938
☐	745		
T	783		
▨	910		
I	912		
▨	970		
▨	3706		
I	3776		

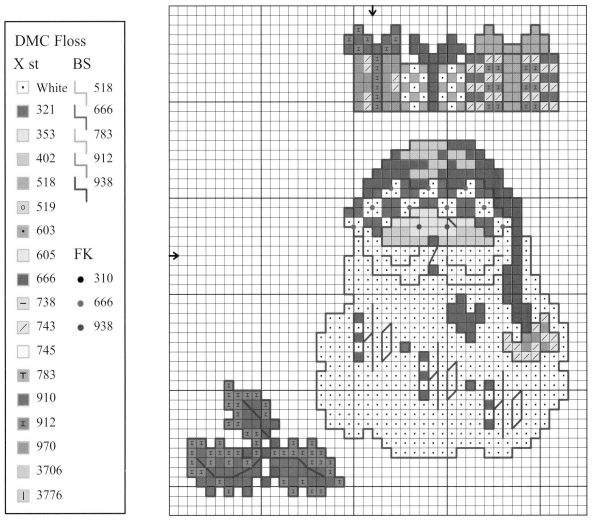

Stitch Count: 24 width x 21 length

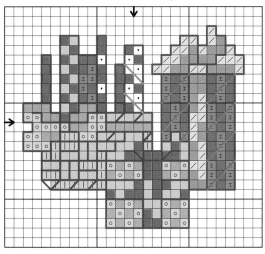

Angel octagonal ornament (as shown on page 115)
Stitch Count: 27 width x 23 length

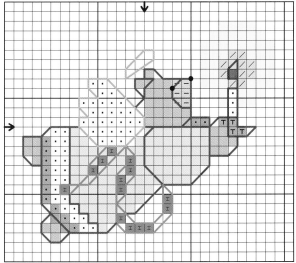

124

Snowman snowflake ornament
(as shown on page 114)
Stitch Count: 21 width x 22 length

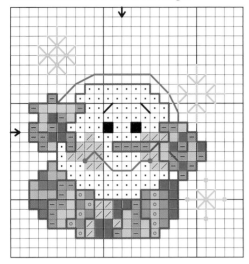

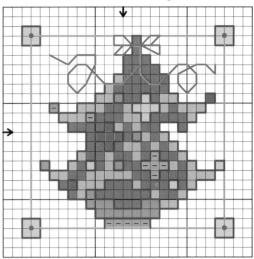

Stitch Count: 22 width x 22 length

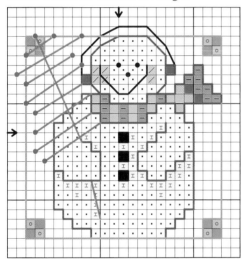

Wreath snowflake ornament
(as shown on page 115)
Stitch Count: 21 width x 23 length

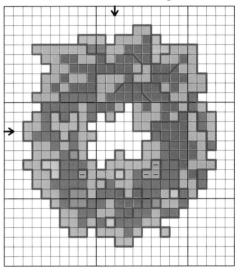

DMC Floss

X st		X st		BS		FK	
·	White		826	⌐	310	●	310
■	310		910	⌐	400	●	666
	666		913	⌐	666	·	813
	725	∧	922	⌐	813		
I	775	–	947	⌐	826		
	783		3705	⌐	910		
○	813	/	3706	⌐	938		

Stitch Count: 20 width x 21 length

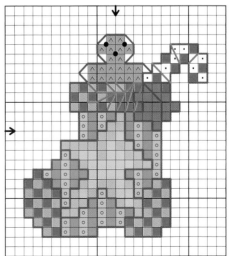

Alphabets

Mug Alphabet

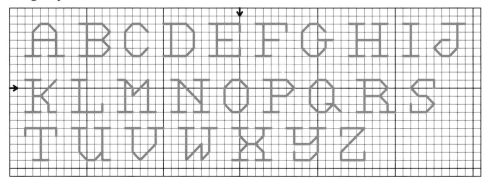

Bookmark Alphabet

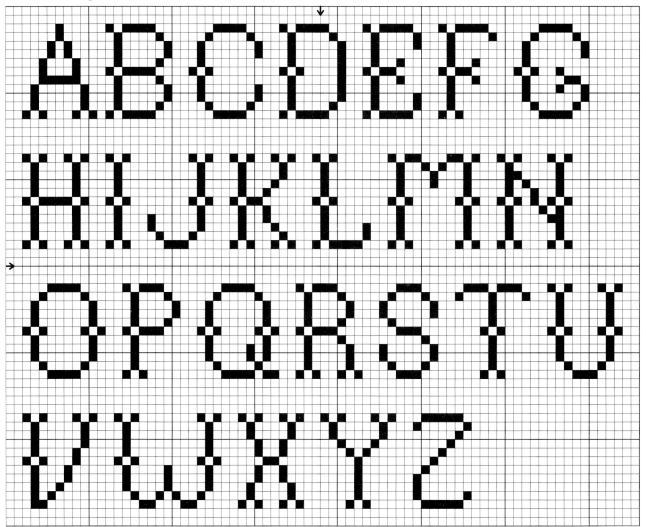

126

Metric Equivalency Chart

mm-millimetres   cm-centimetres
inches to millimetres and centimetres

inches	mm	cm	inches	cm	inches	cm
⅛	3	0.3	9	22.9	30	76.2
¼	6	0.6	10	25.4	31	78.7
⅜	10	1.0	11	27.9	32	81.3
½	13	1.3	12	30.5	33	83.8
⅝	16	1.6	13	33.0	34	86.4
¾	19	1.9	14	35.6	35	88.9
⅞	22	2.2	15	38.1	36	91.4
1	25	2.5	16	40.6	37	94.0
1¼	32	3.2	17	43.2	38	96.5
1½	38	3.8	18	45.7	39	99.1
1¾	44	4.4	19	48.3	40	101.6
2	51	5.1	20	50.8	41	104.1
2½	64	6.4	21	53.3	42	106.7
3	76	7.6	22	55.9	43	109.2
3½	89	8.9	23	58.4	44	111.8
4	102	10.2	24	61.0	45	114.3
4½	114	11.4	25	63.5	46	116.8
5	127	12.7	26	66.0	47	119.4
6	152	15.2	27	68.6	48	121.9
7	178	17.8	28	71.1	49	124.5
8	203	20.3	29	73.7	50	127.0

yards to metres

yards	metres	yards	metres	yards	metres	yards	metres	yards	metres
⅛	0.11	2⅛	1.94	4⅛	3.77	6⅛	5.60	8⅛	7.43
¼	0.23	2¼	2.06	4¼	3.89	6¼	5.72	8¼	7.54
⅜	0.34	2⅜	2.17	4⅜	4.00	6⅜	5.83	8⅜	7.66
½	0.46	2½	2.29	4½	4.11	6½	5.94	8½	7.77
⅝	0.57	2⅝	2.40	4⅝	4.23	6⅝	6.06	8⅝	7.89
¾	0.69	2¾	2.51	4¾	4.34	6¾	6.17	8¾	8.00
⅞	0.80	2⅞	2.63	4⅞	4.46	6⅞	6.29	8⅞	8.12
1	0.91	3	2.74	5	4.57	7	6.40	9	8.23
1⅛	1.03	3⅛	2.86	5⅛	4.69	7⅛	6.52	9⅛	8.34
1¼	1.14	3¼	2.97	5¼	4.80	7¼	6.63	9¼	8.46
1⅜	1.26	3⅜	3.09	5⅜	4.91	7⅜	6.74	9⅜	8.57
1½	1.37	3½	3.20	5½	5.03	7½	6.86	9½	8.69
1⅝	1.49	3⅝	3.31	5⅝	5.14	7⅝	6.97	9⅝	8.80
1¾	1.60	3¾	3.43	5¾	5.26	7¾	7.09	9¾	8.92
1⅞	1.71	3⅞	3.54	5⅞	5.37	7⅞	7.20	9⅞	9.03
2	1.83	4	3.66	6	5.49	8	7.32	10	9.14

Index

1st Place small magnet 93

A Star is Born 13
Alphabets **126**
Angel octagonal ornament 124
Angel oval ornament 116
Angel stocking ornament 118
Apple coaster 62

Backstitch 7
Baker's Rack bookmark 110
Bear & Flower round bib 13
Bear & Goose pocket bib 12
Bear bootie 11
Bear cup 13
Bear mitten 11
Beehive pencil topper 90
Best Friends bookmark 111
Bird keychain 90
Birdhouse bookmark 104
Birdhouse pillow 34
Birds bookmark 113
Blue Gingham ball cap 15
Bookmark Alphabet 126
Bunny pencil topper 89
Butterfly bookmark 105
Butterfly napkin 45
Butterfly place mat 45

Candles heart ornament 123
Carrots jar cover 62
Carrying Floss 7
Centering Design 6
Cherries coaster 62
Cherry Pie jar cover 68
Chilies magnet 98
Chocolates magnet 98
Cleaning Finished Design 7
Cookies kitchen towel 59
Cookies potholder 58
Cross-stitch 7

Daisy fingertip towel 55
Designs for Baby **8–25**
Designs for Bookmarks **100–113**
Designs for Christmas **114–125**
Designs for Jar Covers **60–73**
Designs for Mugs **74–85**
Designs for Pillows **26–37**
Designs for Small
    Accessories **86–99**
Designs for Table Linens **38–49**
Designs for Towels **50–59**
Dove & Heart bookmark 110

Eat Dessert First napkin 47

Eat Dessert First place mat 47

Fabric for Cross-stitch 6
Feather bookmark 102
Feather napkin 40
Feather place mat 40
Finished Design Size 6
Fishing bookmark 102
Floral Heart magnet 97
Floss 6
Flower Basket key ring 97
Flower mitten 10
Flowers & Hearts bath mitt 18
Flowers & Hearts hooded towel . . . 18
Flowers & Hearts round bib 19
Flowers & Hearts square bib 20
French Knot 7
Frog pillow 36
Fruit & Heart jar cover 66
Fruit jar cover 64

General Instructions **6–7**
Geranium jar cover 66
Grapes fingertip towel 54
Grocery List small magnet 92

Harvest jar cover 68
Heart bootie 11
Heart jar cover 63
Heart octagonal ornament 120
Hearts & Stars octagonal
    ornament 118
Hearts, Stars & Candy heart
    ornament 122
Hibiscus fingertip towel 53
Humming Bird magnet 96

I'm a Star bootie 13
Introduction 6

King keychain 89

MOM mug 82
Monogram mug 76
Mouse small magnet 89
Mrs. Mouse magnet 98
Mug Alphabet 126

Needles for Cross-stitch 6
Noah's Ark luggage tag 99
NOEL octagonal ornament 117
Number of Floss Strands 6

Pagoda mug 76
Pansy luggage tag 96
Pansy napkin 42

Pansy place mat 42
Peace and Plenty mug 80
Pear coaster 62
Peas Please kitchen towel 59
Peas Porridge potholder 58
Pencil small magnet 92
Penguin stocking ornament 120
Pink Gingham hooded bath
    towel 10–11
Preparing Fabric 6
Pumpkin jar cover 62

Queen keychain 89

Radishes small magnet 88
Red Berries napkin 48
Red Berries place mat 48
Rose mug 84

Sailboat luggage tag 99
Santa Claus snowflake
    ornament 119
Santa Sign oval ornament 117
Santa snowflake ornament 119
Seasons Greetings fingertip
    towel 57
Securing Floss 7
Shaker Shelf jar cover 69
Snowman oval ornament 117
Snowman snowflake ornament . . . 125
Sports luggage tag 99
Star & Bear burp towel 16
Strawberry jar cover 63
Sugar 'n Spice jar cover 63
Sun & Bear visor 16
Sun keychain 91
Sunflower pillow 29
Sweet Peas mug 85

Teacher pencil topper 92
Teacups mug 84
Teddy Bear stocking ornament . . . 119
To the Beach pillow 28
Topiary bookmark 105

Victorian pillow 33
Vine Flower bonnet 11
Violin towel 52

Water Me pencil topper 92
Watermelon jar cover 62
Watermelon small magnet 88
Welcome fingertip towel 53
When's Lunch? mug 80
White hooded bath towel 14
Wreath snowflake ornament 125